MANIFESTATION CODES: BEYOND LAW OF ATTRACTION

LEARN TO CO-CREATE WITH THE UNIVERSE TO MANIFEST THE LIFE OF YOUR DREAMS, TODAY.

LISA FERNANDES   ALEXANDRA CARRUTHERS
MILLI FOX   KARI RUSSELL   CHARISSA LYNN
ANDI TURCZA

LISA FERNANDES

Copyright © 2023 by Lisa Fernandes

All rights reserved.

No part of this book may be reproduced in any form or by any electronic or mechanical means, including information storage and retrieval systems, without written permission from the author, except for the use of brief quotations in a book review.

CONTENTS

Accessing New Age Manifestation Lisa Fernandes	v
1. THE CODE: THE ART OF STORYTELLING Alexandra Carruthers	1
ACTIVATING THE VORTEX	2
THE BACKSTORY	3
THE PLOT TWIST	6
THE VICTIM	8
THE HEROINE	12
UNLOCKING THE STORYTELLING MANIFESTATION CODE	14
STEP ONE: COMMAND	16
STEP TWO: CRAFT THE NARRATIVE	19
STEP THREE: DEVELOP YOUR CHARACTER	21
STEP FOUR: STORY-TELL WITH ALL YOUR SENSES	23
2. THE CODE: THE INNER CHILD Andi Turcza	27
MANIFESTING THROUGH YOUR INNER CHILD	39
EXPRESS THE EMOTION	39
CREATE THE CONNECTION	41
NURTURE YOURSELF	41
HOW INNER CHILD WORK HELPED ME MANIFEST MY DREAMS	42
3. THE CODE: VISUALIZE, ACT + TRUST Charissa Lynn	47
IT WAS ALWAYS THERE	52
# 1	KNOW IT'S YOURS	53
# 2	VISUALIZE THE DREAM	54
# 3	TRUST THE TIMING	55
# 4	TAKE ALIGNED ACTION	57
A LOOK INTO LIFE TODAY:	58

4. YOUR CHANCE TO INSPIRE OTHERS	62
5. THE CODE: ACTIVATING SELF-EXPRESSION Kari Russell	64
A TURNING POINT	66
THE EVOLUTION	68
UNLOCKING THE CODE	69
SELF EXPRESSION	72
THE THREE PILLARS OF SELF-EXPRESSION	72
Pillar 1: Self-Knowership	73
Pillar 2: Self-Honorship	79
Pillar 3: Self-Ownership	81
The Universe Responds.	84
6. THE CODE: COMPASSION FOCUSED MANIFESTATION Milli Fox	87
Your Source Identity	96
Your Human Identity	97
Your Vortex Identity	99
Self Compassion	102
Self Kindness	103
Common Humanity	103
Mindfulness	103
Self Acceptance	104
Where these Manifestation Codes have taken me:	106
7. FINAL THOUGHTS	111
8. TIME FOR THE WORLD TO MANIFEST	112
About The Authors	115

ACCESSING NEW AGE MANIFESTATION

LISA FERNANDES

I stood in front of a blank wall with a piece of white chalk between my fingertips.

Without thinking, my hand met the cool chalkboard painted wall and began to write. . .

Successful
Trustworthy
Safe
Tall
Handsome
Secure
Healthy
Loyal

My hand stopped when it felt complete. The words scattered in chalk across that wall held more power than I imagined. This newly scripted masterpiece was left for me to see each day. I would walk past them countless times and without knowing, the words became nestled within my subconscious.

Six months later, I experienced my first big manifestation.

I MET MY HUSBAND.

Over the years, I've seen manifestation portrayed in either one of two ways: easy peasy or completely out of reach. Can you relate? We're either told by the experts to keep it simple and just "think positive," or that we need to complete a 100 complicated steps before the universe will respond to our desire.

But what I've realized as I've walked my path is that there isn't a one-size-fits-all approach to manifesting the life of your dreams. We all have a unique relationship with the universe.

Manifestation is like art. When you walk through an art gallery, you see hundreds of canvases filled with different expressions of color and texture. There are thousands of techniques. Some use textiles, others use oils, watercolors or acrylics. Every artist has their own unique way of creating their masterpiece. Manifestation is the same. A teaching that may deeply resonate with and work for you, might not work as well for somebody else. We all have a unique relationship to manifestation that allows us to create masterpieces with our lives.

My intention in putting together Manifestation Codes was to break away from the typical manifestation narratives and open your mind up to possibility, by exploring a variety of embodied practices from a handful of highly successful women.

Throughout this book, you'll be learning from five leaders in the online coaching space who have become masters of manifestation in their personal realities. Each one has a powerful story and practical teaching for you to experiment with in your own life. With each code comes an opportunity to deepen your practice and open up your relationship to universal power.

My hope is that in reading Manifestation Codes, you remember how capable you are of manifesting the life you desire. That you restore your innate worth and co-creative power. And reclaim the magic that has always lived inside of you.

Let's begin.

CHAPTER 1
THE CODE: THE ART OF STORYTELLING
ALEXANDRA CARRUTHERS

It's 6:48 pm. I'm standing in the middle of my walk-in closet, surrounded by the clothes that used to fit me. The hiss of a white noise machine muffles my two-year-old daughter's footsteps. The lights are off and the closet door is open just enough for me to keep track of her as she twirls around my bedroom.

The gentle sound of Brahms' Lullaby soothes my nervous system while I sway in the dark.

"Shhh. Shhh. Shhh," I whisper.

My 4-month-old daughter is almost asleep. Nestled in my arms, her sleepsack tightly swaddled around her chubby little body, I can see her eyelids finally getting heavy. Her long lashes settle against her soft apple cheeks. It's been 25 infinite minutes rocking together in the darkness. And two long weeks of feeling like a single mother.

. . .

My upper back aches. My throat is dry from the constant shhhh-ing.

My boobs hurt. Sweat drips down my temples. The extra fat on my stomach is making me itchy. I can feel the clasp of my nursing bra digging into my skin. There's nothing I can do to adjust it without disturbing Mia. And I'm not about to undo all the time I've spent getting her to fall asleep. So I choose to look at the pain and inconvenient itchiness like a strength test. I've got this.

But my chest tightens and my mind starts to seeth with resentment when I remember where my husband is.

ACTIVATING THE VORTEX

I instantly interrupt the thought.

"I am *not* a victim," I remind myself. Not out loud. Internally, of course. Mia seems like she's finally asleep.

"I am a powerful creator. I command and create my life," I continue the monologue in my mind.

"Every night is getting easier. Dale is healing rapidly. Mia is sleeping longer and deeper. Every day is getting more abundant. Your soul clients are effortlessly finding you. You've already done enough. Money loves you and has got your back. Your body is releasing all its extra weight. It's safe to be supported by others. It's safe to be successful."

. . .

With my eyes closed I create a potent field of focus and I practice engaging as many of my senses as possible in illuminating my vision.

This is my vortex.

The manifestation portal that I enter every night and before each nap. The place where I command my narrative and use my inner eye and voice to consciously craft the sequencing of my life.

Bedtime – once a mundane mom task – has now become a journey into the quantum playground. The place where the first draft of the story I'm about to live is coded and written.

THE BACKSTORY

My shhh-ing gets softer and softer until it stops. The rocking comes to a gentle standstill.

I hold Mia for a few more minutes to make absolutely sure she's resting deeply. I've rushed it before and paid the price of having to start our bedtime ritual of shh-ing and swaying in my dark closet all over again.

I don't think my body can handle another round. And I don't think my toddler, who's now ripping the pillows off my unmade king-size bed, is patient enough either. She's been a trooper through this season of extraordinary change and challenge. But I know her "Chuckie" side, as my husband and I playfully call it, could come out at any moment.

• • •

I watch Mia like a silent hawk, looking for any sign of eyelash flutters or tiny movements that might signal she's not yet descended into her REM sleep. I feel like an expert on child sleep cycles at this stage in the parenting game. Having two baby girls, back-to-back, in a pandemic had me binge reading every piece of baby sleep research on the first five pages of Google, often during the ungodly hours of 2 - 4 a.m., when my little night owlets decided they wanted their boobie buffet.

I can tell you instantly whether a baby is in a true REM cycle or not. And now after 14 days of parenting on my own, I've got my bedtime routine with two girls, two and under, down to an absolute science.

That is until I hear my hyped golden retriever barking downstairs. Fuck.

I panic, but stay completely still. My eyes shoot down at Mia. She didn't seem to hear. Thank God. It's the sign I need to convince me that she's finally ready to be placed in her pack and play for the night. Let's be real, there was no way I was fitting a real crib in here.

I feel bad that we don't have a proper room for her, and that the best I could do was transform my walk-in closet into a tiny makeshift nursery. Mom guilt.

The honest truth is, my pregnancy with Mia took me completely by surprise. More mom guilt.

· · ·

I'd barely caught my breath from her big sister's birth, when Mia's ambitious little Aries soul found a portal into my womb, after forgetting to take my birth control pills for a few days. Yes, more mom guilt.

She was an unexpected blessing that stretched my capacity in ways I was only beginning to discover. The force of nature our family needed to ground and rise into our highest love. A true earth angel.

I gently lay her down and watch her for a minute just to make sure she doesn't jerk awake. Then I tiptoe backwards and slowly open the closet door, just enough to slide out undetected.

I find Charlee playing with some of my make-up in my bathroom. I place my index finger over my lips and signal to her it's time for her bath.

Bedtime routine number two is about to start.

I'm at least 30 minutes out from the only window of alone time I get to enjoy each day. That sacred window between 7:30 and 9 p.m. where, with nobody else's needs to meet, it's just about me.

No babies to hold or feed. No toddler demands to meet. No client messages to respond to.

Just me, and often, the Real Housewives of Whatever-City-Has-The-Latest-Season-Airing.

THE PLOT TWIST

It's during this exact window of time, 14 days earlier, that I hear the front door thrust open and find my husband collapsed, lying on our entry-way rug.

His eyes, wide like a deer in headlights, lock with mine, carrying an expression that simultaneously says I'm fucked. And I'm sorry.

At first, we hope it's just a bad sprain.

He'd come down on the ball wrong playing soccer that evening and heard his leg *snap*.

Unable to walk, his brother carried him off the field and ultimately into our home and onto our couch, the cozy corner of our open concept main floor that would become his home for the next six weeks.

A trip to the emergency room the next morning confirms what we fear most, it's a break. A bad one. He needs surgery immediately. And will have to keep all weight off of his right leg for a two months *minimum*.

Our life already feels like a house of cards.

Our marriage feels shakier than ever. The challenge of having two very young children in the pressure cooker of a pandemic, tense family drama, the rollercoaster of entrepreneurship and reporting on the city's crime beat from home, has us dancing with each other's shadows every other day.

And now, my very hands-on husband and co-parent, is sentenced to spend the next eight weeks with his feet up on the couch. Leaving me to bear the load of caring for our two very young children, three high-maintenance pets and an injured 38-year-old man, while also running the successful business I managed to scale to 5-figure months with a baby on my boob and a toddler running between my legs. Cool.

It's sink or swim.

But the *knowing* is instant.

This tibia plateau fracture isn't random. It's the answer to both of our subconscious prayers. A divinely orchestrated challenge from our higher selves designed to activate the deep codes of potential awaiting to be accessed and awakened in our DNA.

This is our timeline jump. The plot twist we prayed for.

Our opportunity to snap the patterns and abruptly end the storylines of victimhood we'd both been repeating for too long.

As great opportunities often do, it's come in the form of a whopping challenge. A crunchy, uncomfortable set of circum-stances that have shown up to activate and initiate me into the powerful manifestation code I'm going to teach you in this chapter:

How to command your narrative and write your own story. No matter what.

Without this vital code, you can easily find yourself a victim of unforeseeable circumstances. Tossed like a rag-doll in a wild ocean of karmic lessons.

When you embody this code, though, you become the eye of the storm you move through.

You seize the power to choose your role and set your own storyline in motion, no matter how turbulent the sea of circumstance gets. You become the creator of your destiny instead of the heiress of misfortune. You can play any hand the universe deals you and emerge a winner because you know the power isn't in the cards, it's in you.

THE VICTIM

If there was ever a season of my life where I can justify feeling sorry for myself, it's this one.

Past versions of me absolutely did.

After the birth of my first daughter, Charlee, I fell into a deep pit of postpartum anxiety and completely lost my sense of self-identity.

. . .

I always knew I wanted to be a mom.

I'm a natural nurturer who started babysitting at 10 years old. The mama bear in my friends group, who is always making sure everyone feels safe. I adore kids and they love me right back. I hold every baby I'm blessed to meet. So naturally, I thought my initiation into the mom club would be easy.

I spent the first 28 years of my life dreaming up my perfect version of motherhood. A hallmark style movie where I never lost my cool and looked like a very well-rested, perky breasted Greek goddess, taking my baby to cafes and holding her in my lap, while slowly sipping my cappuccino and flipping through pages of a novel. I pictured a peaceful, easeful season of life, where I softened and slowed down. Where bonding with my baby felt effortless and the people I loved swooped in from all angles to care for us. I thought I'd seamlessly return to client work when I felt ready. Effortlessly checking in to support and guide my clients during nap times.

Oh how my own expectations blind sided me.

Nothing can prepare you for the way motherhood rips your heart open. There is no mercy for the initiation this level of love brings. The anxiety I felt was crippling.

I would look at my baby girl's exquisite, beautiful tiny features with a frequency of unconditional love that would fill my cells with a euphoric honey and peace. Only to have my stomach free fall like an elevator with a cable cut, and my mind flood with thoughts of total dread, at the idea that something beyond my control might harm her.

A scene from a child abduction documentary would flash into my awareness. A news story about a child murder. A vision of a car veering off the road crashing into her stroller on the sidewalk.

I'd never experienced paranoia like this before. Triple checking the locks. Calling my husband five minutes after he left to take her for a walk, just to confirm they were both still alive. Struggling to trust even my closest family and friends.

For a while, every day felt so intense.

When you love something this much, you carry the possibility you might lose it too. And that terrified me to my absolute core.

Could I really trust myself to keep her safe in this life?

There were days where I still felt like a little girl too.

My mind buzzed with hyper vigilance. My heart felt raw. My body was exhausted.

The responsibility of protecting my innocent baby girl inside a world matrix that felt increasingly hostile and dark, keeps me anxiously awake during the handful of hours I should be sleeping between nursing sessions.

I feel like a ghost of myself watching every other part of my life come to a complete standstill.

My business is on hold. And I'm full of insecurity and guilt that we're now dependent on my husband to carry the financial load, at a time where we both envisioned being completely financially stable.

I feel like a frozen iceberg in a sea of pressure. And the story I'm telling myself sucks.

My inner narrator spins a tale of a woman who's failed, who's been forgotten, who's not enough for the daughter who's chosen her. She tells me I'm a burden to my family, that my inability to profit on my expected timeline has led us into the fiscal deep end.

I believe every word.

The tiny fear that lived in the back of my mind for years is now a self-fulfilling prophecy.

I'm telling myself a story I don't want to live: the struggling mother and failing entrepreneur.

. . .

Playing the role I don't want to play: the victim of circumstance.

Until something finally *snaps*.

My husband's right leg.

THE HEROINE

The night my husband breaks his leg is the plot twist my story needs for my character to develop into the heroine she knows she's here to be.

It's the night I make the choice to command my own narrative. To consciously direct my energy into weaving together the life I want to live and the story I want to one day tell my daughters, about who their mother is, and more importantly who she became for her family during this chapter of intense challenge.

With nobody coming to rescue me, I evolve my inner princess into a queen. I start to get crystal clear on how this storyline is going to play out. I vow to emerge from this with everything I want.

I remember telling my husband on the phone when he wakes up from surgery that this is going to be the catalyst for incredible new things for both of us. That God is giving this *to* us, as a gift, on opportunity and portal to actualizing our higher potential.

. . .

The strength and conviction in my voice comforts and inspires him.

He feels it too. And he decides, on the record, that he's going to have the fastest and fullest recovery his doctors have ever seen.

I decide I'm going to be an exceptionally attuned mother, a graceful wife and focused boss in business who settles for nothing but passionate profits.

I start to craft the story of a woman who rises no matter what. Who sees every challenge as a catalyst. Who doesn't allow a tough set of circumstances to set her back one inch, but chooses to use it as the accelerant that propels her toward her dreams at warp speed.

I hire support and allow myself to receive more from loved ones. I get very intentional about the clients I desire to work with and my capacity. I redesign elements of my business to support my vision. I use my voice and actions daily to affirm my success.

With a 4-month-old, I'm living on a 24 hour cycle. There's very little downtime. So I choose to get disciplined and creative. My biggest manifestation hack is using ordinary moments of motherhood to consciously create magic.

My daughter's bedtime routine becomes my most potent portal for manifesting.

. . .

The task I used to dread the most, quickly becomes one of the most sacred and powerful time slots in my day. Where I drop into a deep zone of focus, deliberately and intentionally weaving together the story of my inevitable success.

My walk-in closet/nursery becomes the vortex.

My dark womb of creation, where the formless dreams and visions of my desires first take form through the thoughts and commandments of inner voice.

While I rock and shhh my infant daughter, I fall into a deep trance state. I focus and speak my visions into existence with a high degree of clarity and intention. I engage as many of my senses as I possibly can, while speaking to myself in the third person. Telling myself the story of what I want to experience in my business, in my marriage, as a mother.

It's inside this quantum playground, where I really begin to understand the important role storytelling plays in manifestation. I unlock the deeper meaning of language and words, and begin a majestic initiation into the power of my voice.

And hone my own storytelling manifestation process.

UNLOCKING THE STORYTELLING MANIFESTATION CODE

You see words are not just words, they are codes.

. . .

Every word carries an energetic essence. They are like keys of sound and light that unlock doors of understanding and consciousness. The words we repeat on loop in the theater of our mind form the primary narrative upon which we build our life. We are the creator. Our thoughts and our voice are the instruments we use to direct frequency into form.

When you remember the holy power of your words, it seems so simple.

But language is a tool that can both liberate and limit.

Many of us are unaware of the mighty manifestational charge our words carry because we're born into a matrix that uses language to manipulate and distort the pure truth of our creative potential.

From the moment our soul chooses human life, our programming through language begins. In the womb, we absorb the sound of our mother's voice and the frequency of her thoughts into our tiny bodies as they develop cell by cell. This forms the bedrock of our self-perception and becomes the spine of the story we'll spend the next couple decades of our life telling ourselves.

As we grow up in the physical world, our indoctrination deepens. The words and tone of our caregivers, teachers, friends, media and culture form the beliefs, principles and concepts that create our entire reality and sense of self.

. . .

As children, we believe exactly what we are told.

And this continues into adulthood until each of us reaches our own unique moment of awakening – where PLOT TWIST – we remember that we are actually responsible for creating our life and start to command a new narrative and write a different story.

In the same way we can program with language, we can deprogram.
    We can use the power of words to instil new belief systems that set us up to succeed in our own sacred way.

We must tell ourselves the story we want to live. And command the narrative of our own life. We must use our words to consciously build the construct we want to live in.

When my husband's leg snapped, so did my victim narrative. I stopped looking for anything outside of myself to rescue me and chose to step into my power to command my life to start forming in my favor.

That meant getting used to speaking in a whole different tone.

STEP ONE: COMMAND

The first step to manifesting through storytelling is to get comfortable commanding.

. . .

Commanding is on a totally different frequency than asking. When you command, you are certain you are going to receive what you are seeking. It's not up for question. It simply is.

To command your narrative means to create from your inner god or goddess. It means to live, speak and move from the purest part of yourself. The part that knows who she is, what she wants, what she deserves and the limitless capabilities of her creation.

To command, we must break the codependent relationship many of us are programmed to have with God, the universe or any higher power. We must deprogram the parts of our psyche that believe something outside of us determines our ability to receive exactly what we desire.

We don't have to ask for what we want. We simply have to command it.

The electrons in this universe rearrange themselves through the power of our focused intention.

When we use potent words to firmly command in our own voice, the outcomes we want to experience crystallize into form - its universal law. We truly speak life into existence.

When we command, our sound comes from a deeper part of our being. There is no wobble, no shake, no doubt. Just pure creative power.

. . .

When I *command*, I can feel the source of my sound emanating straight from my womb. My voice has a deeper, more powerful tone.

It's louder. It's certain.

When I *ask*, my sound comes only from my throat. My voice is higher and shakier in tone. It seeks permission and is definitely not certain.

When you're struggling to manifest, check-in with your tone. Are you asking an outside power to grant your wish? Or are you commanding electrons like the queen of source energy that you are?

Our power to manifest comes down to the level of intention and conviction we hold when we speak.

The electrons in the universe respond to our commandments, not our questions.

The tone of voice you use to manifest and storytell matters. It's the foundational key. You could craft the most exquisite storyline and get hyper clear on what you desire to manifest in your reality, but if your voice is cracking and your heart is asking, then the electrons just aren't getting the memo to get into formation.

. . .

The more comfortable you are at commanding your life and speaking with divine conviction, the more mighty your manifestational power becomes.

We can command without uttering a sound, too. Commanding has nothing to do with volume, and everything to do with power and intention.

In the quiet darkness of my walk-in closet, while rocking my daughter to sleep, I'd enter a deep trance and speak my story into existence just using my inner voice. I could feel my body respond differently when I'd start to command. My cells would activate in response and I'd feel a rush of sensation build and swirl throughout different energy centers in my body.

Commanding in silence became my speciality. Every night I restructured my reality.

STEP TWO: CRAFT THE NARRATIVE

Once we've nailed our tone and gotten more accustomed to commanding, it's time to get clear on our story. What exactly do we want to create?

Without realizing it, many of us are actively playing roles inside narratives we'd rather not be in.

We are living out stories we wish we could change, without seeing the ways we internally speak them into being every day. When we blame, complain or tell ourselves some outside force is in control of a key aspect of our desired destiny, we are actively writing ourselves into a storyline we don't want to experience.

It's easy to find yourself living out a victim drama. In our modern matrix, there are many outside forces trying to hook you into narratives of powerlessness so they can profit off your self-perceived lack.

After my first daughter was born, I found myself living out the story of the struggling new mom and business owner. With my second daughter, I chose a different narrative to craft. In the sacred darkness of my walk-in closet, I spoke into existence a story of wild success, extraordinary grace and a woman who beat the odds to create the life she wanted.

When it comes to manifesting through storytelling, we must be highly conscious, intentional and focused on crafting the narrative we desire to experience. We must only subscribe to stories that empower us and lead us towards the successful outcomes we want to manifest in all aspects of our life.

I had to stop buying into the stories society tried to sell me about motherhood and entrepreneurship, and consciously command and craft the story I wanted to tell about my journey.

This is an advanced step of reprogramming our consciousness through intentional language, that has everlasting benefits in our sovereign ability to manifest life into form and create our own reality, free from interference.

· · ·

The more specific, deliberate and intentional we are in weaving together the plot line of our life and choosing the words that best illuminate the essence of our desires, the more we will see these frequencies crystallize into form around us.

It took a spicy life crisis to snap me out of my victim narrative, but that doesn't have to be the case for you.

Any ordinary life moment can become the plot twist that sets you on a new path. Any decision can be the choice that has you jump timelines and line-up instantly with the calling of your heart.

What's most important is seizing our creative power and scripting the life we want to live, with love, vivid detail and joyful excitement. And to ensure we cast ourselves in a starring role.

STEP THREE: DEVELOP YOUR CHARACTER

The character we choose to play in our story, has a massive impact on our manifestations. We can't assign ourselves the role of the victim and reap the rewards of the queen.

We have to get conscious about the character we're developing and how specifically we're developing her. What traits must she embody to succeed in her mission? What shadow patterns must she overcome? What is it time to heal? What must she now release? What skills is she ready to master?

. . .

I got crystal clear on the woman I was going to become as I led myself, my family and my clients during this chapter of personal challenge. Powerful, graceful and incredibly successful. The type of woman who wins every day because of her attitude and passion for the game of life.

I let go of waiting for someone to rescue me and assumed complete responsibility for every element of my life. I stopped complaining. I gave myself grace to fully feel the intensity of my emotions, but didn't create a whole story around them.

I overcame my reactivity and calmed my anxiety. Every toddler tantrum was an opportunity to practice gentle parenting – with my kids and myself. Every argument with my husband was a chance to practice loving communication and relationship repair. Every bill was a way to cycle money with gratitude.

I actively began to heal my codependent inner little girl. I stopped making her wrong for feeling overwhelmed. I validated her and cultivated an inner mother who could soothe her and talk her down with a calm, assertive tone. I showed her how it was safe to follow her inner truth, even if that meant being disliked along the way. I stopped grasping to relationships that were already crumbling.

I let go of identifying as the martyr. I asked for help and actively built a team of support staff, a therapist and mentors to hold me, while I was holding it down for my family and my business.

And I started to master a new level of emotional intelligence and abundant thinking. The word "lack" completely exited my inner discourse. Everything was either a direct blessing, or a lesson that led to a blessing.

This new version of me had a direct impact on the floodgates of abundance that began to pour into my world.

Most nights, I'd come downstairs after my bedtime manifestation ritual, check my phone and find payment notifications from new women signing up for my offers, direct messages from followers interested in working together, or messages from other entrepreneurs wanting to join forces or invite me to share my codes with their community.

My business was blowing up, in a good way. Not one ball dropped. My income and impact continued to grow. All because of the character I decided to play in the story I was consciously coding.

Conscious character development is a vital piece of the manifestation puzzle. It's through our inner language and outer actions that we shape ourselves into people who are actually capable of holding and managing the scope of our manifestations.

STEP FOUR: STORY-TELL WITH ALL YOUR SENSES

The final piece of the storytelling manifestation code is unlocked in the details. The vivid, descriptive elements you weave together to illuminate your narrative of success.

. . .

Deep in my closet trance, I'd engage all of my senses in my storytelling manifestation sessions.

I'd use my imagination to paint an intricate picture of what I wanted to experience. I'd use my inner voice to command with conviction. My inner ears could hear the recognition and praise coming from the future testimonials from my clients. My tongue would literally salivate as my inner mouth would taste the exquisite celebratory meal I'd visualize eating after hitting a new financial milestone. My heart would melt like warm butter as I'd feel the joy of walking along the beach as a family.

I went deep into the details. Immersing all of my senses into the art of storytelling. Directing all of my focus towards consciously creating - through my mind and voice - the life I was about to experience.

The richer the details, the richer the experience, the richer the manifestation. Letting your imagination run wild by infusing every element of your story with decadent depth is how you supercharge it.

I still continue to harvest fruit from many of the seeds I planted during my quantum storytelling sessions in the vortex. Clients who are still growing with me today. Mentors who've opened up a whole new spiritual world. Friends that feel like sisters. This book project. Being just a few.

And even though many of my manifestations look different or come in unexpected forms and timelines, they're the byproduct of the level of focused energy I generated through engaging all of my senses.

The more vibrant and delicious my vision, the more enjoyable the experience is when it lands.

By immersing yourself fully into the depths of the details, you bend the laws of time and co-create the most exquisite outcomes.

During those two months of crisis, I used the power of storytelling to transform myself into an extraordinary woman. A graceful mother, a fire business woman and a devoted wife.

I calmly led my family through a turbulent chapter, ensuring my home was a healing sanctuary full of love, warmth and nourishment. And that my daughters had an attuned, empathetic mother to calibrate to each day.

I grew my business by 100% while working only 8 hours a week. I built a support network of incredible allies and cultivated extraordinary relationships. I met a new edge of my leadership and sharpened my brand and craft.

I deepened my intimate relationship with my husband. His fall literally became my rise. And the healing crises we needed to bring more of our individuality to our union and our love.

. . .

His doctors told him that his recovery time was the fastest they'd ever seen. He was back on the soccer field within months, and his body has never felt stronger.

You have the power at any moment to start to speak a new life into existence. The world around you is created in the studio of your mind through the sounds of your own inner narrator. If it's not the plot line you want to be living, it's up to you to ignite a plot twist.

A whole new dimension of your manifesting abilities will unlock as you harness the creative potential of storytelling.

Commanding your narrative, crafting your own storyline, developing your character and engaging all of your senses, are the skills you need to become the director of your reality and the manifestor of your heart's wildest desires.

If you don't love the story you're in right now.

Turn the page. And simply start writing a new one.

CHAPTER 2
THE CODE: THE INNER CHILD
ANDI TURCZA

Breathe, Andi.

Just breathe.

I can hear my heart pounding and my thoughts spiraling out of control, as I pace back and forth down my hallway, nine months pregnant. This is it, my baby is coming.

I'm terrified. Tears rolling down my cheeks. NO.

I try to swallow the fear, but I can't.

I've taken all the classes and I've read all the books, but nothing prepared me for this and I'm scared to my core. I've failed at virtually everything in my life. And I don't want to fail at becoming a mother now. It's been three years since I last spoke to my dad, but I can hear the sound of his voice playing on a loop in the back of my mind, as if he's standing right behind me.

"You're stupid! You can't do anything right."

It's like his words are burnt into my brain.

Feeling a surge of terror, I ask myself, "Is this what it feels like jumping out of a plane? No. This has to be worse. Why am I so scared? Millions of women have babies every day. This must be normal, maybe I'm not normal?"

I question myself as the shame creeps in and mixes with the terror. Then I quickly try to reassure myself, but it's too late. The anxiety takes over, and I just let it rip.

There's no turning back now.

I'm on my way to the hospital, still unclear and unable to process what's happening. Nine months didn't feel like enough time. Then it hits me: I'm absolutely petrified to become a mother.

The hospital stay feels cold, long and exhausting. I'm given every single drug you can think of. They tell me to hold my breath and stay still, as they inject my epidural into my spine. Six minutes, that feels like an absolute eternity.

. . .

I feel so alone. So scared. So many thoughts racing. The medication starts to kick in and now I feel numb. I push for hours, and eventually, my 9 pound 2 ounce baby boy arrives. He's crying and healthy with 10 fingers and 10 toes, everything perfectly in place. We name him Antonio.

The relief of his healthy delivery doesn't last long.

"How in the world am I going to do this?"

The fear floods my system with full force, like a water dam exploding. I can't get my dad's voice out of my head.

"You're so stupid. You're such a failure."

The terror grows stronger as I know in my gut I won't have help from anyone since I'm such a stupid failure. At this point it hasn't occurred to me that my dad was wrong. I still believe everything he said about me.

Just breathe Andi, just keep breathing.

The next few weeks at home with my newborn are a sleepless blur. I can't recognize my reflection. It's an intense whirlwind. I turn to God. Even though I'm not spiritual at all, I'm desperate for some sort of higher power to fill me with hope.

. . .

My husband and I are on shaky grounds, and things are getting worse fast. I've got no energy left for him. He blames me for everything that goes wrong. And I feel so angry, sad, scared and alone. I lose my temper all the time. I scream and yell at him to try to get him to do more. I apologize immediately, telling him I'm overwhelmed and tired, that I don't mean the awful things I'm saying, but that I'm desperate for his help that never seems to come.

With every outburst, I immediately regret it. Apologize. Beg for forgiveness.

"I'm so stupid. My dad is right again."

Everything feels like my responsibility. My husband seems to have nothing to do with the baby, the house, and the bills. Don't I have the right to get upset here? I love my husband so much, and up until my son was born, I did everything for him. Yet I'm slowly recognizing how little I get back in return. Still it feels like I can't leave.

It's the middle of the night when I hear Antonio cry. I'm seething with resentment as I get up to feed him. I feel so mad that nothing that I asked was done yet again that day, so I mutter something rude as I walk out of the room. When I reach Antonio's crib, I take a deep breath and scoop him up. It feels peaceful here. Late November, the middle of the night. I grab a small blanket and drape it over my shoulders. My baby's only three weeks old, and I absolutely love these quiet, snuggly moments together.

• • •

As I'm breastfeeding, I look out the window into the dark night. There are only a couple of stars in the sky tonight. I stare at them, as I let myself get completely lost in the spiral of my thoughts.

"Why isn't my husband more supportive? Why isn't he more present? Why doesn't he want to be part of the feedings? Why doesn't he want to smell and stare at the baby? What am I doing wrong? Maybe he doesn't love me."

Shame and guilt strike me hard.

"Maybe I'm too fat. Too ugly. How can I fix this? How can I protect my baby and not feel like this anymore? What if I can do more? I envisioned having a baby surrounded by love. I envisioned us doing everything together. My husband is only growing more and more distant, there is always something wrong. He isn't happy."

All of a sudden the door opens and my husband walks in, sits next to me and confirms what my mind already knows is true: he's not happy.

Here it is, I think. He wants to leave me.

I look at him with tired eyes and say, "Do you think this is the right time to talk about this?"

Then he blurts out, "I need more! I need more from this marriage!"

. . .

I look down at my precious baby and then I look back up at him and say,

"How much more can I possibly give you? I just gave you a child."

It's at this moment, he asks for a threesome.

This changes everything for me.

I grip my baby tighter. Tears roll down my cheeks. *What the hell is wrong with him? What did I do to deserve this?* This wasn't the first time he's mentioned this, but I always ignore it, hoping it would just go away. *Why wasn't I enough for him? I just gave him the best gift anyone could give, and he's sitting here saying he won't be happy until I give him more?* I'm disgusted. I'm sad. And I can feel myself becoming depressed. All I want to do is take care of my baby.

After that night, I start to develop a deep hatred for my husband, but choose to ignore the truth and lie to myself about it. I don't feel good enough for anyone else. I don't want to end up divorced like my parents. It feels like I have no choice but to stay with him, so I avoid my feelings at all costs.

I spend my days feeling sorry for myself and praying to God that something changes and somehow it all works out. We never speak about that night again. It seems like a bad dream, one I'll never forget.

. . .

The next year's full of disappointment, as I willingly keep taking the blame for everything. My husband comes and goes as he pleases. He continues with his lifestyle, his friends, and his sports, as I'm left home alone caring for our baby. It's far from the perfect family life I'd envisioned. I yell and cry, but he's always so calm and just points out how crazy I am. And I slowly believe him more and more.

My pain becomes my deep dark secret. No one knows how bad it is. I always put on a smile and pretend everything's good, but the truth is I'm dying on the inside. No one knows I physically hate him. No one knows the only reason I continue to live is because of my precious son.

My pretending gets so good. Not only do I convince myself, I also convince my husband that we're a perfect couple. He tells me nothing would make him happier than having another baby, and of course I believe him.

This is my chance. We will be so perfect. Just the four of us.

December 25 2013.

Off to the hospital we go.

This time things are different. I don't practice my breathing. I'm way more confident. I'm stronger. I'm mentally prepared. And I have a plan. I show up at the hospital and immediately tell them I don't want any drugs during my labor. I take control.

. . .

A few hours in, I think I might have made a mistake. But things move quickly. The pain is intense, but I focus. I've got this, I tell myself. It's the most physical pain I've felt in my life, but in command of my body and calm.

I push three times. And in just 15 minutes, I'm done. My plan works. With no epidural, no drugs, totally aware of every sensation I birth my 11 pound, 2 ounce baby boy Michelangelo into the world.

Holding my new baby boy for the first time, I feel relief.

But it's not long before my anxiety creeps in. I tell myself it's from the noise around me. I shake my head, hoping that it will shake off the nervous energy, but it doesn't. I keep thinking noooo not this feeling again. I'm calm! I'm ready! Not today! But the anxiety stays put.

Then it hits me: I have two baby boys now.

Once I get home, things get interesting. Antonio, now two-years-old, calls me as I'm feeding Michelangelo.

"Where's their dad?"

He's not present, as usual, and full blown anxiety smacks me.

. . .

"What the hell am I going to do? Split myself in half? How in the world am I going to do this alone?"

My biggest fear is coming true. Consciously, I want to believe my husband is going to support me this time, but deep down I know he isn't. No matter how much I plead, whether I'm nice or rude, I know all he cares about is sex, friends and soccer. He doesn't really care about me. And that's when I find myself in denial. I keep seeing flashes of my parents divorcing in my mind. I shake my head no. I tell myself we'll never split up.

So I simply become a single mom who lives with her husband. He stops being a part of anything we do and I get tired of fighting with him. He doesn't want to contribute to anything and always makes me feel bad for asking him to be part of outings. It feels like I can't go on like this. Begging him to take out the trash. Begging him to cut the grass. Begging him to help with diapers. Begging him to go to work. The tasks are endless. I know marriage isn't easy, but this feels ridiculous. Like I married a lazy child.

He keeps telling me he loves me, even though it doesn't feel like love. I believe his lies, or at least I really want them to be true. I feel confused around him.

He often says things that make me question reality. He tells me that my feelings aren't valid and that I'm imagining things. He speaks so calmly and nicely to me, I believe him. And I seriously start to think I'm losing my mind.

. . .

It's now 2016, and after years of countless fights, I beg him to go to couples therapy. He refuses. And this brings me back to six-years-old, hearing my parents fight. I hated it. And I realize that I don't want to raise my kids in the same environment. This awakening pushes me to get help and I begin going to therapy alone, a decision that changes the trajectory of my life forever.

I start learning about narcissistic abuse and it's like suddenly everything I've been experiencing in my marriage starts to make sense. I'm sad because I can now clearly see his manipulation tactics. But I also feel excited and happy in a way, to finally have my sanity back.

For the next two years, I study everything I can about narcissism.

I read books and research articles, devour YouTube videos and learn from other people's struggles online. I relate so much to everything, and start to become aware of the narcissistic patterns playing out in our relationship. I start to change the way I respond and I stop allowing him to manipulate me.

I throw myself into self-love, self-respect, self-worth books and meditations and I begin to truly heal. I find my inner source of love and unravel the patterns that landed me here. I stop allowing him to feed on me, and finally get the courage to leave our marriage.

In 2019, he moves out.

. . .

I'm free.

And it feels exhilarating.

After he's gone, I realize just how heavy and oppressive his energy felt all those years. I stop feeling scared all the time. And eventually, the anger and hatred dissipate too. I come to a place where I just want peace. I'm done with the nonsense stories, lies, manipulation, gas lighting and love bombing. I want to show my sons, now five and seven, what healthy love is like.

And I realize, while I've found my way out, that it's important to understand how I found my way inside our toxic marriage to begin with. I need to understand how I married a narcissist.

While studying narcissism, I recognize the same patterns and traits my husband displayed in our marriage, my mom also had growing up. I feel mind blown. It's a huge breakthrough. My entire life flashes before me. So many memories of being gaslit, dismissed and manipulated. *"You're crazy. You don't really feel that way. You must just be imagining things."*

Everything makes sense now. I ended up with a narcissist, because that's what love felt like to me. He treated me exactly the way my mom treated me. A part of me feels relieved to finally get to the root of the pattern, while another feels daunted by the long road of healing and recovering ahead of me.

I decide it's time to start taking responsibility for everything in my life. I start to see my people pleasing personality coming out everywhere. But now I understand it isn't truly serving me. It doesn't actually keep me safe. My desire to fix broken people, my constant need for love and my over apologetic nature isn't because of other people, but because of how I feel about myself.

When the pandemic hits I spend my time in and out of lockdown with my kids and dogs rebuilding my life. Inside this cocoon, I'm led to one of the most important facets of my healing journey: my own inner child.

Finding her is another life altering moment.

Discovering that all of my feelings are actually valid and that my triggers simply show me where I have an inner child wound to heal, shifts everything for me. I learn the art of forgiveness. And I forgive myself. I see the ways that I didn't value myself and how the universe reflected this wound back to me through my partner.

That all along there's been a hurt little girl inside of me calling out for love.

Unearthing my inner child helps me find the gift in my divorce. Even with all the pain, anger and years of suffering, I feel deeply grateful, because unpacking it all was the catalyst for so much growth, expansion and healing.

Because of my divorce and the lessons that came with it, I finally feel like I can truly love myself. And this has filled me with the desire to help other people too.

MANIFESTING THROUGH YOUR INNER CHILD

Today I work as a quantum manifestation coach, and inner child healing is a big part of what I teach my clients. It's an important piece of the manifestation puzzle.

When we talk about inner child healing, we're talking about healing the little person inside of you. Close your eyes for a second and imagine yourself at five-years-old. It might feel like this version of you is just a memory from the past, but what many of us don't realize is that our inner children are very much alive inside of us. Sometimes they're even the ones running the show, especially when we have unresolved pain. When we connect with our inner children and give them the chance to fully express themselves, the pain that we've been carrying inside all these years alchemizes and transforms, freeing up more energy to create and manifest with.

EXPRESS THE EMOTION

When I work with my clients I take them back with a series of questions to provoke memories of discomfort, sadness, anger, frustration, hate, guilt, grief etc… Then I work with them to identify the emotion associated with the memory. The intention is to zero in on the trapped feeling and give it the space and opportunity to be fully felt.

If your mom never allowed you to express yourself as a little girl and always dismissed how you felt, instead of yelling at her as an adult and saying this is how you should have treated me, you give your inner little girl a chance to express her feelings.

. . .

Here's an example from my own childhood. Growing up, I hated meat, but my mother always made me eat it and would gaslight me and tell me I liked it.

In a healing session around this memory my inner six-year-old would say, *"Mommy you're so mean! I feel the way I feel! Stop telling me I can't feel this. Stop telling how I'm supposed to feel. It makes me feel sad. It makes me angry. Stop saying I like meat when I keep telling you I don't! I hate you. You don't know how I feel!"*

I give my inner little girl a chance to express her feelings in full. I don't edit her, censor her or hold back. If she needs to scream, kick, jump or stomp, I let her. The goal is to let all of the feelings out.

You can use a pillow or a chair and pretend that pillow or chair is your mom or dad or brother, sister, or whoever it is that you want to express your feelings to, and allow that little person inside of you to speak and fully express herself.

Say whatever it takes to release the pain that you've been holding on to all these years. This is so therapeutic because you're acknowledging that little person's feelings for the first time. And when you do this, something magical happens. You release all of your pain. You'll know you've let most of it go when you feel like there's nothing left to say. It's like a natural sense of completion washes over you. When you feel this, you're ready for the next step: forgiveness.

Forgiveness is a whole different lesson on its own. You might feel ready to forgive, and the words will easily flow from your heart. Or you might not feel fully ready yet and that's okay, even stating that you want to forgive somebody opens up space for healing and release. The universe will take care of the rest.

CREATE THE CONNECTION

Next you want to create a connection between your adult self and your inner child. With your eyes closed see yourself as an adult and get on your knees and give your little person a hug, look them in the eyes and say I love you, I am here for you and I am going to support you always. Going forward, have their picture somewhere you will see it everyday and consciously check in with them. There might be times where more healing and releasing are required.

Every time you look in the mirror, say, "I love you," because you're not just saying it to your adult self, you're saying it to the inner child inside who desires nothing, but love and self-expression.

And every time you feel the urge to talk negatively to yourself, remember you're also saying those words to your inner child. Every single time you put yourself down, every single time you call yourself stupid, you're actually talking to that cute little person within. They hear everything.

NURTURE YOURSELF

The more you nurture your inner child, the more you increase your capacity to live fully and manifest powerfully in your life. Connect with them daily. Ask them what they want to eat, where they want to go and what they want to do. Let them have some fun! I can't tell you how much joy and vitality this unlocks. It changes your whole vibration, which makes it so much easier to resonate at the frequency of your desires.

It's also important that you begin to use your triggers as opportunities to reparent your inner child. Anytime you feel fear, sadness, anger, remember these feelings are acceptable and normal. Simply acknowledge them, express them and feel them fully. Remind your inner child, that you're here to protect them, that you have their back, and watch how quickly your nervous system calms down.

HOW INNER CHILD WORK HELPED ME MANIFEST MY DREAMS

I've become a whole new woman thanks to healing my inner children. I love all parts of me. I feel a natural confidence. I know how to set and hold healthy boundaries. I've made peace with my past and continue to heal my trauma as it shows up.

I've gone from being a stay-at-home mom in a miserable marriage to single mom running two businesses, something I'd never imagined myself to be capable of before healing my inner children. I'm fully in command of my life now. My schedule is flexible, so I'm always available for my kids. I love my clients. And the work I do fulfills me on a soul level. My life is a dream come true.

I acknowledge and accept all my emotions. I no longer make myself wrong for feeling them. I now understand that our emotions are our guidance system. I live my truth and show up unapologetically and authentically me, without worrying about whether people are going to like me or not. I no longer go out of my way to please others. This is a big one for me. Instead I tune into what I desire and what my body needs from me. My feelings come first and then I make a decision from there.

I choose peace over drama daily. I choose me before anyone else. This new version of me is truly manifesting a life to be proud of and the best part is I know it's really only the beginning of my story. With this newfound power, there are no limits to what I can create with my life.

Here's a small taste of the magic I've been manifesting through my inner little girl.

One Friday night in late 2022, I was laughing with a friend and I shared how badly I wanted to move because our current townhouse had too many stairs. We laughed it off and forgot about it. But the following Monday my landlord asked me to move! I was shocked. What did I do, I thought? I manifested this and wasn't even sure I was ready to leave. I really wasn't in the position to move financially. I should have been devastated, but I trusted I was being divinely guided.

Some fear creeped in and now when I feel it, I welcome it. I simply gave myself the permission to feel my feelings for one afternoon. That's right. I gave myself one afternoon to cry it all out.

Then the next day I get to work, grab my favorite journal and write out exactly what I want and need for my family. I don't allow myself to get deterred by the tough rental market, or the fear people project onto me. 13 days later, I find my dream place with an amazing new landlord. The move cost $7000, with first and last month's rent. Cue my anxiety. But instead of panicking or pushing it down, I feel it fully, pray to God and go to bed.

The very next day, my landlord messages me, saying, "You were the best tenant I ever had. I'm so sorry, I had to ask you to move. I will pay for your first and last month's rent." The universe always delivers!

At this time, I'm driving a 2016 Nissan Rogue, and it starts to give me trouble. Nothing major, just wear and tear, but it felt annoying constantly having to take it into the mechanic. In just a few months I spent $2000 on repairs and I'd had enough. I released my emotions and asked the universe to take care of it, fully trusting it would all work out.

On my drive home, I call my friend and tell her I'm done going to the mechanic.

"It's time for the universe to send me a new car," I say half joking.

We both laugh, and I completely forget about it.

But the very next day, I get a call from the dealership. It's a Saturday evening and I have a few friends over, so I put the phone on speaker.

. . .

"Congratulations," the lady on the other end of the line says. "You've won a free upgrade!"

Now I really thought it was a joke. But she was dead serious.

One week later, on the same day I'm supposed to bring my car into the shop for a repair, I drive away in my new 2019 Nissan Rogue. The perfect upgrade, delivered right on divine time by the universe.

The impossible was becoming possible for me. I'll share one more.

After manifesting my new home and car, a friend asks me to cat sit for him. I say yes! The job is five days long. But that's all it takes for me to fall completely in love with Pepper. When he comes to pick him up I feel totally devastated. I can't understand what's going on with me, but I allow myself to feel my emotions and connect to my inner little girl.

One night I was joking with my friends and I said out loud how I just wished my friend would give me Pepper. It felt like an impossible wish. I mean, who would just give away their beloved pet? I made peace with the fact that the cat wasn't going to be mine, and opened my heart up to the idea of getting a different cat. I wrote a letter to the universe asking it to send our family the perfect pet.

. . .

One week later, my friend messages me and asks me if I want Pepper. I'm completely shocked. *Did I literally just manifest the impossible? How is this happening?!*

My answer is a full body yes.

Our family manifested the perfect pet.

And my inner little girl is absolutely filled with joy.

CHAPTER 3
THE CODE: VISUALIZE, ACT + TRUST

CHARISSA LYNN

The house was still dark, our little black and white shih tzu Charlie was scratching at the door barking to be let in from the ice cold rain pouring down. My once hot cup of tea was getting colder by the minute. The curtains were open but the sun had not come up yet, as the world was waiting for the day to begin, mine was already underway.

My baby was making little cooing sounds as I changed his diaper. I gently laid him on his back and watched as he kicked and squealed in delight at the nursery rhymes playing joyfully from his musical play mat. I decided to skip our usual tummy-time. It wasn't his favorite and, honestly, mine either. I always tried to avoid the possibility of disaster early in the morning. Who wants to start the day with a baby crying and a three-year-old toddler spilling cereal milk all over her lap? I already felt like a zombie. With kids this young, survival was my main focus, whatever the cost.

I was scrolling social media mindlessly like most wanna-be-sane mothers do. Finding a way to escape the mundane everyday tasks of parenting two little ones. When something caught my eye. I stopped scrolling instantly and saw a post that stood out like a diamond amongst a pile of black carbon copy coal pieces. On the surface, it was nothing impressive. But it totally captured my attention.

"Look at what my friend is selling. Bath bombs. Her business is blowing up!"

I looked at the poorly lit photo of handmade green bath bombs, tied up in a crinkled plastic cellophane bag with low-quality lime green ribbons frayed at the ends. The bath bombs were laid out on a white plastic tray, as if to say "come get me" or "I may be cheap but it's better than nothing."

My instant egotistical reaction was, "I can do better than that."

Now don't get me wrong, it was incredible that this social media friend-of-a-friend had taken the time to create a product by hand and then had the courage to sell it. I'd give her a trophy if I had one. She clearly had a bravery that most don't possess. She had an idea and she actually acted on it. Seeing her post activated something deep within me. I knew that if this woman was making a "killing" from simply hand-crafting fizzy citric acid balls, with a splash of let's stain your bathtub leprechaun green, then I, a Kindergarten teacher, with two kids tied to her hip, using caffeine and toothpicks to keep her eyes open, could sure as hell do the same.

With confidence and a go-getter attitude like mine, I knew with certainty that I would blow hers out of the water. I knew that I could do it too, but only a trillion times better. I felt like I could make this into something massive, in a way that ordinary play-it-safe humans would never attempt to do. And so I did.

Looking back, that morning scrolling social media was divine intervention. It was the perfect beginning to a mind-bending manifestation story.

Two months earlier...

"Babe, come up with an idea," my husband Andrew blurted out to me in a half joking manner.

You know the kind statement your partner makes, where they don't really mean it, but at the same time they're like, come on, let's go, I'll let you save the day? Yep, that was the kind of innocent verbal message that came out of his mouth on that lame Friday night. Andrew and I, both young parents, were watching Shark Tank as our form of entertainment, while still grieving our pre-baby late nights drinking at the infamous London, Ontario, downtown bar Joe Kools. That's exactly where we met, swaying together on the overcrowded dance floor before heading out into the night linking arms on the downtown streets after hours, while I belted out the new hit song by Rihanna, "We Found Love." We stuffed our faces with hot gooey pizza, completely oblivious to the fact that one day in the not-too-distant future we'd be married with kids. But that's another story for another day. For now, let's carry on with this one.

"Let's be millionaires", my husband said nonchalantly.
• • •

Our 3-year-old daughter Lia had just fallen asleep. I was rocking our baby Jaxon in the wooden rocking chair, wearing my usual polyester stretched and stained pajamas, the only ones that fit me at three months postpartum. I was hoping Jaxon would stay asleep long enough so that Andrew and I could enjoy a quiet evening together indulging in our usually Friday night routine: Shark Tank.

We loved watching these ambitious wannabe entrepreneurs perform their rehearsed pitches in front of a line-up of billionaire investors in hopes that they'd cough up the kind of capital and expertise that could take their business to the next level.

It was the type of show that most ordinary people watch, their faces turning green with envy, while they kick themselves in the ass thinking, *"Why the hell didn't I think of that?"* Or even better, look at their partner like mine did, and ask, "Why didn't *you* think of that?" As Andrew, always the jokester, loved to do on the regular.

But this night was different, instead of my usual eye rolls and sarcastic comebacks, a feeling came over me. I felt this rush in my body and heard a soft voice whisper to me, *"ya, why don't you come up with something Charissa?"* And so I hit the drawing board. I didn't know it then, but that night I opened the door to manifesting my own million dollar company, in a way I never could've predicted.

"I can do better than that," I repeated to myself, this time with much more conviction.

. . .

I'd been trying to come up with an innovative business idea day after day, but nothing felt promising enough to take action on. A couple nights later, during another one of our lame Shark Tank Fridays, I said to my husband, "How about a snappy bracelet that forms to your wrist with a pen at the end of it? Every junior kid in the school would love this invention! A bracelet that turns into a pen."

But as a teacher it didn't take me long to realize that this wasn't the best idea. Kids might poke themselves accidentally and snappy bracelets are noisy and distracting. Yikes. I kept racking my brain, trying to force a creative idea to come. I so badly wanted to become one of those entrepreneurs making millions.

A part of me was still in shock that this virtual stranger was making a fortune from selling her unappealing green bath bombs. I couldn't shake it. I felt like I'd been divinely guided to her photo that dark winter morning. Maybe this was my million dollar opportunity? I decided to do some research.

I swiped open the browser on my phone and typed into the Google search bar "how to make bath bombs." I'd never made a beauty product in my life, but I had this fire and excitement in my body I couldn't ignore. You know the kind where your intuition is screaming "do it" and your human self is trying to decide if it's brave enough to actually follow it? That's the type of fire I'm talking about. I was full of courage that day. I chose to listen to my intuition and I took action.

"Could this be my million dollar move?" I dared to dream out loud.

. . .

Little did I know that I was on the pathway to manifesting exactly what I wanted.

IT WAS ALWAYS THERE

Growing up, I wasn't raised to think big with money. My parents were middle class. My step dad worked long hours flooring homes, wearing down his knees with every passing moment, swearing to my three brothers and I, that one day he would win the lottery and we'd be rich. My mom was an at home child care provider, teacher and insanely talented artist, who sold her art on the side. I was brought up with the mentality of you've got to work hard for what you want in life and even then, you still might not always get it. It was a very play-it-safe kind of upbringing. I was taught to be cautious of what the future holds, leading me to many years of being fear ridden, afraid I'd make a move that might lead to a financial disaster.

I had no idea about the law of attraction. The concept that my thoughts and beliefs created my reality was totally foreign to me. But I did feel this unexplainable innate knowing deep inside. A part of me understood that I could get whatever I wanted out of my life and that nothing could truly stop me.

For years, I was completely oblivious to the fact that I held this knowledge within me. For a long time my manifestation codes were present but dormant, just waiting for me to press play and activate them. And so I did.

In a few short years I went from being an anxious 25-year-old who doubted she'd ever find the man of her dreams, to marrying my soulmate and building our beautiful family together. I also started and scaled two incredibly successful companies.

. . .

That idea I had to make lip balms that night watching Shark Tank?

Well, I did it.

I'm now the CEO of the million dollar product company, Crushed. We sell our aftercare beauty products all over the world. I also run a multi-six figure coaching company, where I mentor women on how to start and scale their own businesses.

I manifested my dream life using the manifestation codes I'm going to break down for you in this chapter. Apply them to your own dreams and watch the magic unfold.

1 | KNOW IT'S YOURS

Manifesting the thing that you want can only happen if you truly believe that it can be yours. Now this is hard for most people to accept because their life is filled with evidence of all the times they didn't get what they wanted. And so many people have created a belief system that operates on the premise that receiving what you desire is in the hands of fate alone.

The truth of the matter is, you can have anything you want if you believe it's yours. When you know for certain that it's yours, it's only a matter of time before it shows up in reality. I like to call this the *certainty frequency*. This is where your mind, body and soul are all in a state where they are 100% sure that this dream is yours, no matter what. When your own energetic frequency is in a state of complete certainty you become an energetic match for receiving that in your reality.

Think of your energetic system as a radio station. You know you want to marry the man of your dreams, have the kids, the white picket fence, the perfect job. This reality exists on the frequency of 111.1. But, your own thoughts, beliefs and actions don't vibrate at a frequency that matches this station. You're currently operating on the frequency of 77.7. In your current reality you're dating men who lack commitment, you feel like your biological clock is ticking, and you're stuck inside your miserable teaching job. Sound familiar?

The only way to manifest the dream life you want is to start living and broadcasting *that* frequency. This is where the certainty comes in. To experience the 111.1 frequency, you've got to consciously attune to it. You've got to get your mind, body and soul in alignment with it. If you don't consciously take command of your frequency, your life will feel like it's full of static, or worse, you might end up attuning to 98.1, the old folks easy listening station, and end up manifesting the complete opposite of what you truly desire. It's important to clean up any sort of wobble, disbelief or uncertainty in your energetic field, because it impacts your frequency. Certainty and *knowing* that what you desire is already yours, is the first key to manifesting exactly what you want.

2 | VISUALIZE THE DREAM

The next key is to harness the power of visualization. When you visualize your dream unfolding, with the kind of depth and detail that makes you *feel* like it's actually happening, you create a power field for manifestation. I remember when I was making my hand-made bath bombs, lip balms and soap for Crushed Aftercare Inc., in my basement at home, I kept visualizing myself having an actual production space outside of the house. I envisioned employees supporting me inside a beautiful facility. I saw it so clearly that I had excitedly said to my business friend one day, "It's as if it's happened before."

I believe that in that moment, when I was seeing it all unfold in my mind's eye, that I was accessing another dimensional field where this desire of mine was happening on another timeline. And it was up to me to adjust my energetic frequency so that it was a match for that exact reality. This may sound a bit *woo woo*, but trust me. And if you believe in multiple realities of existence, I know you already get it.

Your subconscious mind doesn't know the difference between reality and fiction, this is what makes visualization so powerful. You aren't just dreaming, when you take the time to envision with depth and detail, you are co-creating. When you know with certainty it belongs to you, you consciously focus on it daily with your minds eye, the next manifestation code comes into play: to trust the divine timing of it all.

3 | TRUST THE TIMING

"Be patient, my grasshopper," my business coach told me just over a year ago.

"WTF," I thought inside. The last thing I wanted to hear was to be patient. I was ambitious, hungry and wanted it all now. I had the attitude of a little girl stomping her feet at the local fair, demanding she get her oversized stuffed animal prize before she's even handed over her ticket to play the shoot-the-duck game. Yep, that was me alright.

When it comes to manifesting the things I really want, patience is a practice. I've gotten better at doing my part and surrendering the rest to let the Universe do the heavy lifting. I try to remain open and allow myself to be pleasantly surprised with the timing of my manifestations. I've also learned that sometimes what we *think* we want, isn't it. And by not delivering our initial desire, the universe is helping us unlock the deeper one. For example, I may think I want to manifest a black Mercedes convertible, but the universe knows I hate it when the wind blasts my hair and turns it into a gnarly rats nest. So by not giving me the convertible, she has my back, leading me to contemplate at a deeper level what it is I truly want: a sleek black Mercedes with a roof. Can you tell I'm totally in the midst of manifesting my dream car?

It's important you have full faith and trust the timing of your manifestation. It's your job to know the what and the why, but it's the Universe's job to orchestrate the how and the when. This is the heavy lifting. Remember, I knew I wanted to make a killing from making bath bombs too, but I had no idea how it would happen, and I sure as hell didn't know it would turn into a company that makes branded aftercare for tattoo artists and permanent makeup artists all over the globe. But here we are! Everything I desired was delivered by the universe, in its own divine timing.

But don't think you're getting off that easy. Yes, the universe will divinely deliver opportunities, open doors and lead people into your life at the perfect moment, but it won't roll out the red carpet and drag you down it without any of your own personal effort. It's your job to take aligned action. Your manifestation won't just magically appear on your lap. One of my favorite quotes by the late Wayne Dyer is: *"There is no law of attraction without action,"* which leads us perfectly into our next key.

4 | TAKE ALIGNED ACTION

Now this concept of taking action can ruffle some feathers, especially if you believe in only following what feels good for you 100% of the time. Listen, I fully believe you should follow your emotional guidance system, but resistance is part of being human. Sometimes the actions our intuitive guidance nudges us to take are going to feel uncomfortable. Do you know how many times I've *not* wanted to press the live button on my phone and talk to the entire world? Too many to count! But, despite my sweaty pits and blotchy red neck, I did it. I took the action the universe guided me to take. I was nervous, awkward and so uncomfortable, but it was so worth it. I developed a vital skill that created thousands of connections for my business. If I stayed idling in my comfort zone, I never would've manifested all of the incredible opportunities that have come through both my businesses.

There are going to be times in your manifestation journey, where you're going to have to make choices and take the steps to actually create the outcome you want. Sometimes these steps are going to be uncomfortable. But we are on this earth to grow and develop. You have talents, skills, perseverance and physical capabilities that you are very much meant to use in our three dimensional world. When we take action, our mental wish becomes a tangible result. You can't expect to become a super fit runner if all you do is stare at marathon racers on your vision board, while you eat chips and binge Netflix. You've actually got to get up and run.

. . .

Manifesting the reality that you want comes down to seeing yourself as the master creator of your own life and taking action each day towards your desires. Now I don't mean just throw spaghetti at the wall aimlessly taking every single action possible. This is where your intuition and logic can work together to lead you down the path of least resistance. Choose to listen to what feels good, what lights you up, the messages that your intuition is sending you daily, but also taking action that is intentional and strategically makes sense to get you one step closer to your manifestation. If you do this, it's truly only a matter of time before your manifestation comes into form.

A LOOK INTO LIFE TODAY:

Back when I was 30 and single, I'd describe my dating life to curious minds – like my Uncle Garth, who wondered how a woman my age could possibly function without a man – and tell people I felt like a princess who kept kissing frogs, waiting for her prince. I'd dated a handful of men that year and nothing felt right. I was a frustrated independent woman who knew exactly what she wanted, but couldn't find it. Until I picked up a book that changed my life, *He's Just Not That Into You*. Everyone remembers that book right? They turned it into a Blockbuster movie! Reading this book made me feel like a powerhouse woman. I was done putting up with bullshit excuses from guys with commitment issues. I claimed my inner Queen and was ready to call in my King.

And that's exactly what I did. I read the book. Slammed it down, scaring the bejesus out of my new shih tzu puppy Charlie, and then chose to believe in my own worthiness. I made a definitive decision that changed everything: I was no longer going to chase my future husband. I would no longer chase the dream. And with this new found knowingness and certainty, my dream man landed in my lap months later on the Joe Kool's dance floor.

. . .

We got married, had three beautiful children, moved into a million dollar home in our dream neighborhood, and quit our government jobs to run two very successful businesses. We fell in love and became bosses on our own terms.

When I look back on my manifestation journey, I realize that it was the certainty I had in myself and my desires that helped me co-create the life of my dreams. I had the desire. I saw the vision. I claimed my worth and then I held the certainty frequency of "this will be mine" and then it was. But all of these manifestations didn't come without setbacks, doubt or fear or anxious thoughts. There are so many times I was terrified to make the wrong move.

Visualization felt natural to me, but patience was difficult to embody. *Trusting the timing* has been the most challenging manifestation code for me to embody. I manifested my family with Andrew so quickly – we were literally pregnant with our daughter three months after the night we met and moved into our house together six months later, that had this expectation that everything *should* come quickly. My ambitious soul wanted every desire to come just as fast. But what I've learned on my path is that everything happens on its own divine timeline. Part of the manifestation process is cultivating the trust and patience to believe it's working, even when you can't see it.

There is so much more that I desire for the success of both of my businesses. I can see it and feel it all so clearly. *Visualization code?* Check. I want both of my businesses to continue to to expand, I want to write my own business book, to be a world renown coach and business leader, to have sold out programs, masterminds and private coaching spaces, to travel while working, to expand our production space and team, and the list goes on and on.

But for now, I am going to hold that vision, to have full faith and 100% certainty that it will happen, and then to do the hardest part of surrendering to the magic and divine timing of the universe.

Everything I have ever wanted has come to be and everything I now want to manifest is coming to me, this I know for certain. These manifestation codes I've shared work with universal law. If you follow them, your manifestations will unfold.

I got it all. You get to have it all.

Believe it.

See it.

Claim it.

Trust it.

And go get it.

. . .

Now it's your turn to write your own mind-bending manifestation story. I dare you.

CHAPTER 4
YOUR CHANCE TO INSPIRE OTHERS

"Nothing is impossible. The word itself says 'I'm possible!'"

— *AUDREY HEPBURN*

My goal in writing this book is to inspire you to manifest what may seem impossible. It's to show you that when your mind, body, and heart are in line, those things that seem out-of-reach, really aren't.]

I hope you're already feeling that inspiration, and that, page by page, you're expanding your mindset and allowing the evidence of manifestations instil the potential within you.

Inspiration is powerful… and this is your opportunity to pass it on to someone else.

. . .

The beauty is that you don't yet have to have completed your own manifestation to inspire someone else to begin theirs... All you have to do is share with them your motivation and the things driving you.

And you can do that right now simply by writing a few sentences.

By leaving a review of this book on Amazon, you can inspire someone else to know manifestation is not only possible for everyone but can feel and look entirely normal.

How? When you let other readers know how this book has inspired you and what they'll find within its pages, you'll show them where they can find the same inspiration that kickstarted you on your journey to epic manifestations.

Thank you for helping me on my own manifestation - to show everyone that they can achieve their dreams and manifest a life they love with ease. Inspiration is a powerful tool; when we share it, we can help each other take the steps we need to achieve anything we desire.

Add a review link QR code here.
  Hyperlink the section **"By leaving a review of this book on Amazon"** *with* **your** *review link.*

CHAPTER 5
THE CODE: ACTIVATING SELF-EXPRESSION
KARI RUSSELL

From the beginning, and I mean the very beginning of my existence, I wanted my presence known and felt. During my birth on February 1st 1983, I almost killed my mom. Don't worry, she's still very much alive and well. I came into this world with the power of a lion, and the impact on my mom was intense. She had a near death experience and spent the first 48 hours of my life, fighting for her own in intensive care.

I was two days old when we were finally introduced, and my mom totally thought somebody switched babies on her while she was recovering. In her own words, I looked like a toddler, not a newborn. I was big. She even needed my dad's confirmation that yes, I was indeed her daughter. My mom and dad would joke that I looked like a baby body builder, I had a lot of muscle on my newborn frame. The fact that my body was "bigger" always seemed to be a topic of conversation inside my head. It was something that caused a lot of contradictory feelings of shame and pride in my self-esteem and self-expression as I got older.

. . .

In all honesty, I had a fucking amazing childhood. Sure there were challenges but my parents were both very present and supportive in my life and I knew every single day that I was loved.

I was a ham in front of the camera, always wanting to be the center of attention, coming up with dances and performances at family gatherings. I was the kid, who in Grade 2 was the emcee at the school Christmas concert. I never shied away from the spotlight. And growing up as a middle child, I was definitely the "wild one" in the family, always testing the boundaries of my expression.

As I grew up, I hit puberty at a very young age. I was the first girl in my Grade 4 class to get her period, wear a bra, sport stretch marks, hips, cellulite and thunder thighs. Remember, I was a "big" baby, and that translated into me being a "big" kid. Hitting puberty had me gaining weight and the curves that come with it by Grade 5. And it was at this time that I started to become very self-conscious and stopped feeling the joy I once felt in the spotlight. I started hiding. I started dimming. I started trying to fit in instead of stand out. I developed severe acne and my skin became a major pain point in my self-image. I remember being called "moguls" because of how bumpy my skin looked. As soon as I was allowed to wear makeup, I never left the house without a full face on. Covering-up my insecurities with false confidence was something I excelled at. I don't think anyone around me, even my family and best friend, would have ever called me self-conscious.

I was really good at faking it.

. . .

I had created a persona based on what I thought would be most accepted by those I was trying to impress. I started to care more about being seen a certain way, rather than being seen as myself. I based all my preferences on what my current friend group was into. Dressing like them, listening to the same music they listened to, heck I even tried to be a skater girl because one of my boyfriends was a big skateboarder and I wanted to be "cool" enough for him.

Over the years this pattern continued and I became less connected to the truth of who I was. I felt ashamed and afraid that I'd be judged, so I continued to keep a lot of my authentic self *hidden*. Like pretending that I was studying religion class at school, so I wouldn't get funny looks while I was secretly learning about Wicca and Spirituality. I didn't have the confidence to stand firmly in my authentic power, so I ended up making a lot of decisions based on what I thought I should do, or had to do, to fit in and make other people happy.

A TURNING POINT

It wasn't until I became a mom and had my daughter Addison, that I realized I needed to heal my inner shit in order for there to be a safe space for her to be herself. How could I tell her she was perfect if I didn't first believe that myself?

It was at this time in my life that I started doing deep reflection work and found *The Desire Map* by Danielle Laporte. Which honestly, completely triggered the fuck out of me by the way. It made me aware of how disconnected I was to my body and my truth. Even the word "desire" made me cringe and feel uncomfortable. I had associated the word with physical and sexual desire, and because of the lack of self-confidence in my body, I was completely detached from the word and my expression of it.

It was this exact discomfort I used to go deeper into why I was feeling that way, and how it had impacted my presence in the world. As uncomfortable as I felt, I was deeply drawn to understanding myself at a deeper level.

I became obsessed with all things personal development, mindset and self-exploration. I took every personality test out there, read so many books on finding your strengths and participated in weekend self-development workshops.

When I found Human Design in 2018, it was as though my entire existence finally made sense. Every fear and limiting belief could be linked to the conditioning of my undefined centers. Everything started falling into place and I realized how misaligned I'd become. I'd been going through life trying to prove myself, and change myself to fit in.

It's a really humbling experience when you realize you've been your own biggest bully your whole life, allowing outside influences and the need for external validation to be your guiding force.

As I started to know myself again, the word desire no longer caused me discomfort. I allowed my big dreams to be seen and felt, and I started to feel alive again. I began to connect with my sacral and heal my self-perception. I started to see the impact I had on others and began attracting opportunities to live a bigger, more fully and authentically expressed life.

I started seeing myself as a worthy investment and a spark ignited inside. I remembered that little spitfire of a girl, the one who thrived being the center of attention, who wanted all eyes on her, because she knew she was here to be seen and felt in the world. I knew my authentic expression is something worth exposing and putting on display, to show others that their authentic expression is the key to living a life they absolutely fucking love!

Over the next few years I'd learn everything I could about myself, my mindset, my emotional intelligence and Human Design to understand how I was meant to be showing up in the world, and the specific thoughts/feelings/beliefs that were holding me back from truly unleashing my authenticity. I wanted to understand how I best manifested and received all the desires I was no longer scared to admit I had out loud. I also got certified in Human Design to be able to bring this potent work to my clients. It was through this investigative process, I realized what had been missing from my life was my pure self-expression. It was time to not just to remember who I was, but to unapologetically express myself in everything I did. My new belief became: *Self-Expression Is Everything. And Everything Is Self-Expression.*

THE EVOLUTION

Self-Expression, and the three inner pillars that I will share with you in this chapter, became the foundation of my growth and evolution. The process that I continue to use to play at the edges of my expression in life and business. It's the process that has helped reshape the view of my body. I've healed (and continue to heal) the wounds around my "thunder thighs," my skin, my stretch marks and my presence in general. I now see my body as the canvas that I get to create art with through my expression.

· · ·

Authentic, bold expression is now the foundation of my business and what people hire me to coach them on. I get to create incredible experiences for people in my community to come back to themselves and be who they truly came here to be.

It's through this process that I can now confidently stand behind what I know to be true for myself, as I continue to expand and activate others through my authentic expression. I do this by going first, by being the leader I'm here to be, consciously choosing to know myself better, to honour myself more deeply and to unapologetically own the fuck out of who I am, so I can empower those around me to give themselves the permission to do the same.

UNLOCKING THE CODE

What I'm about to share with you is actually quite simple, and something you're probably already doing, but aren't consciously aware of. But, before I go into explaining what it is and how to use it, I want to give you some context around how this code came to be, and how I embodied it in my life. This code isn't a *"doing"* code. It won't require you to buy anything or to learn anything overly complex. This is a tangible code that you can integrate into your daily life immediately.

The thing is it will ask you to be incredibly *vulnerable* and *honest* with yourself. This may bring up some past traumas and triggers that will create feelings of discomfort and unease, and I want you to know that it's ok to feel all the feels, and to lead yourself to getting the support you need if it becomes more than you feel like you can hold on your own. You should know that in my world, we embrace discomfort. We trust that even when we're playing at our edges, we're still safe. We utilize tools and strategies to continue to grow, despite the discomfort we feel. We use fear as fuel to propel us forward in the direction of our desires. Desire will play a BIG role in your ability to leverage this manifestation code in your own life.

It's important to note, I will never ask you to abandon your truth, but rather ask you to be open to shifting your perspective to see how playing with this code could potentially elevate your experience in life. Because when I get to the heart and soul of this code, my biggest desire for you is that this practice allows you to experience even more freedom, liberation, pleasure and joy in all areas of your life and business. Because if it doesn't feel good, then what's the fucking point right?! Right. Ok, let's go!

I guess it's time I properly introduce myself. I am Kari Russell. A wildly audacious and spicy 5/1 Sacral Generator who is obsessed with the work that I get to do and the impact I get to make. Over the last 5 years I've built a million dollar brand that generates multiple six figures per year as an Energetic Business Coach. I work with leaders in the entrepreneurial space to own their power, leverage their authenticity and express themselves boldly and unapologetically, while they build their business their way.

My coaching style fuses Human Design, mindset work, emotional intelligence, spirit and self-expression so my clients can create massive impact and unimaginable income, in pure unadulterated alignment and integrity with who they are and what they want. In my world we play big, we get loud, we take up space, and we stand in deep self-leadership and personal responsibility, which is an integral piece of the manifestation code I'll be teaching later on.

· · ·

I'm now 40-years-old, and I want to say that it took me 35 years of trial and error to truly find myself and my "thing." I've literally had every kind of job under the sun from dog walking, tutoring, working at a dry cleaners, a sports store, Tim Hortons, to office management, marketing coordinator, bookkeeper, advertising rep, to personal trainer and nutrition coach, to assistant manager at a luxury retail brand to life and goal coaching, to going back to school at 33-years-old become a teacher only leave the classroom 18 months later to go all in on my business. Yes. I've truly been a jack of all trades. It's what I had to do, while I was in the process of figuring out who I was, what I wanted, and how I wanted to experience my life. And through this experimental journey, I endured a ton of shame for not being able to "stick to one thing" and had this feeling that I was behind in life because I wasn't committed to a single career path.Why is this important to share with you? Because I want to show you that part of the manifestation process is being honest with ourselves, and allowing the truth of what we are making things mean to come to the surface.

This code requires you to have deep trust in yourself, even when the steps you're taking don't look "normal" or "consistent" with what you see others doing in their lives. We still experience a lot of conditioning, shame and guilt around experimentation and bouncing from thing to thing, which can lead us to neglecting our soul's mission and, instead, falling into the trap of just doing what's considered "safe" or "expected" of us, compromising our true desires.

When I look back on my journey in hindsight, I can clearly see that all of these experiences were part of what led me to the awareness of the manifestation code that I'm teaching you today, and helped me to find and acknowledge a major piece of my identity and purpose for being here. So, grab your journal, and get ready to dive into the manifestation code of self-expression. The more you embody it, the more co-creative power you will unlock to build the life of your dreams. Are you ready?

SELF EXPRESSION

This manifestation code is rooted in *authentic self-expression*. For most of us, our relationship to self-expression is based on our past conditioning and our fears, primarily our fear of being judged or rejected. We tend to go through life picking up everyone else's ideas, opinions and beliefs around what's acceptable and what's considered "normal" or "safe" based on societal and familial pressures and expectations. We become disconnected from who we actually are in the pursuit of fitting in or being seen a certain way. Our soul is suffocating under the pressure to keep up with everyone around us. And if you're reading this book, I know you desire more. A lot more. Which means, on some level, there is also a desire for more freedom in your expression. This manifestation code will help you bring back those feelings of freedom, liberation, pleasure and joy in your experience of life, and business, that you've been seeking.

So, let's dive into the three key pillars of self-expression, so you can manifest the life and business that your heart deeply desires.

THE THREE PILLARS OF SELF-EXPRESSION

Each of these three pillars requires a level of self-awareness and self-reflection in order for you to truly harness their manifesting power. Like I said before, you don't need to really *do* anything, but you must have a willingness to go beneath the surface of who you've always been and consistently ask yourself, *"am I expressing who I truly am, or who I think I need to be?"*

• • •

My suggestion, grab a journal (or the accompanying workbook) and create the space to truly investigate each of these pillars. If you want to elevate the experience even more, take yourself out on a solo date to your favorite coffee shop or restaurant, grab a drink you love, and create an atmosphere of celebration for leading yourself through this work. It's the commitment to continual conscious awareness of intentionally expressing who you are through each of these pillars that will have you manifesting the life and business you desire.

PILLAR 1: SELF-KNOWERSHIP

Do you know who you are?

Not who you've been told to be.

Not who you think you should be.

But who you came here to be?

We begin here, and continue to revisit this pillar as we grow and evolve. This is where you get radically honest with yourself about uncovering where you've been holding back by not fully acknowledging who you are as an individual. We can't authentically express ourselves if we don't know who the fuck we are. And we surely can't express ourselves or if we're trying to be someone we're not, especially when it's from a place of people-pleasing or peace-keeping.

Self-knowership is where you meet yourself over and over again, uncovering deeper layers of your identity and your desires. This is where you unlock those differentiated distinctions that make you who you are, and that give you the keys to how you're meant to show up and express yourself in the world. It's through the exploration of what makes you, *you,* and the releasing of all the shit you've picked up along the way, that allows the purity of who you are to be seen and experienced, not only for yourself, but for everyone around you. This is a declaration to becoming the living, breathing, embodiment of who you came here to be, which in turn gives those around you the permission to be their full selves as well.

So, who are you? *Really.*

What do you stand for? What comes naturally to you? What lights you up? What are your strengths? What are your truths? What do you desire out of life? How do you best communicate? What impact are you here to make? What skills and expertise do you have? What are you *best* at?

Initially, these questions may create more confusion than clarity for you. For me, I know before I found Human Design, I wouldn't have been able to answer them myself, at least not with the same certainty and conviction I can now. I'm aware that Human Design is a multi-layered system that can be quite overwhelming, and not everyone resonates with it, but if you're curious and want to investigate your energetic blueprint, head to mybodygraph.com to grab your free chart (you'll need your birthdate, birth time and birth location). I'm going to break down the five main Human Design types with some tangible tips. If you feel called, find out yours and then come back to this chapter.

. . .

Manifestors:

Your magic is truly rooted in your unfiltered, unadulterated, unapologetic authenticity. You don't need permission or validation - you need to trust your desires. You're here to wildly activate those around you with your eccentricity and big vision. Your energy is radically sporadic and can fluctuate from very high energy to very low energy, often with no rhyme or reason. Don't let the conditioning of society tell you you're been too much or too lazy - your rhythm is perfect for you.

Even though you don't *need* anyone or anything to make shit happen, you're not here to do it all on your own. Ask for the support and look to build a community of people around you who can help bring your vision to life. Remember, you're not here to be told what to do, so ensure you're able to execute without needing permission from anyone else.

The World Will Tell You: Your energy is too big and your ideas are too wild. That you move too fast and that you're not moving fast enough.

What You Need To Remember: All you need is self-trust. You don't need your ideas validated or permission granted for your desires. Trust yourself, and you'll be golden.

Generators:

As important as it is to follow your sacral *yes*, honoring your sacral *no* is just as impactful. You'll best connect to your sacral with closed ended questions like "*yes* or *no*" or "*this* or *that*." Tighten up those boundaries and watch the opportunities that light you up roll in! Yes, you may be the *workers* of the world, but that doesn't mean you're here to do it all. You're here for mastery over a lifetime, so look for common themes in all the experiences that light you up and follow that sacral flame. Your radiant energy will naturally attract and magnetize people and opportunities when you follow your joy. If it doesn't light you up, you're the wrong person for the job. Let your bold confidence be seen and felt. You know what you're good at, so own it fully and flaunt it.

The World Will Tell You: You can do it all. You can handle it. You've got the energy.

What You Need To Remember: Just because you can do it, doesn't mean it's genuinely in your highest interest. If you don't *desire* it, then don't do it. Move with your sacral *yes*, and don't override your *no*.

Manifesting Generators:

You're actually here to be too much! Quit dimming yourself down to make others feel comfortable in your energy, they need you to light their path. Be all the things and do all the things. This is your magic! Your path won't look linear or normal to the outside world. People will question you and your ability to handle it all, but that's your jam, you are the master multi-tasker.

You're here to try everything and anything your sacral leads you to, even when it doesn't make logical sense. And for the love of life, stop feeling shame for not "sticking it out" or "following through," you're built to start and stop. You're here to grab the lessons you need, and move on to the next thing. Drop the people pleasing and peacekeeping and let your desires lead the way.

The World Will Tell You: You're too much, too all over the place, too scattered.

What You Need To Remember: Being *too much* is your gift. You're not here to make others comfortable, you're here to be all of you and trust the right people will flock.

Projectors:

Your power activates those around you. It's time to strip back all the doubt and fear and let yourself be seen in all your glory. You're not here to move in the same way or at the same speed as everyone else. Your energy is stable and consistent, yet it's not regenerative. You need plenty of downtime to rest and recharge.

Don't get caught up in the rat race of life trying to keep up with those around you. You're not designed to run the race, you're the one laying the path for others to follow. The natural leader, coach, mentor. The guide in you needs to feel seen and recognized for the value you offer, don't feel shame or guilt for needing this attention. This is your clue that you are being invited into the aligned opportunities for you.

. . .

The World Will Tell You: To keep up. To work harder. To move faster.

What You Need To Remember: When you make *smart* moves, you end up being more efficient and effective than most people. Use your power of probing focus. It's truly quality over quantity for you.

Reflectors:

Your open energy draws people in. They feel your wisdom and intuition, so ensure you're navigating your environments and surrounding yourself with only things that make you feel good.

You will naturally experience highs and lows in your energy. You'll feel like the star of the party one day, and then want to hide in hermit mode the next. This is perfect for you as you will absorb the energy and emotions of everyone around you, letting you taste and play in different people's aura. Your time in solitude is integral in remaining aligned and true to you. You're here to take your time and feel into the decisions you make and the moves you take, so don't let the pressures or expectations of others rush you. Your ability to reflect back to the world what you feel and see will be radically mutative for those around you. Ensure that your boundaries are solid and that you're only choosing to be in spaces that feel nourishing. You're not too picky or high maintenance, your energy is the greatest commodity and prioritizing it is your number one asset.

The World Will Tell You: You're too sensitive. You're too inconsistent. You're too unpredictable.

. . .

What You Need To Remember: Surprise and delight is your magic, baby. You're the unicorn of the world. Rare and unique in all you do. Trust your energy and your speed. It's all perfect for you.

Now, Human Design isn't the be-all-and-end-all of Self-Knowership. I'm sure some of you are also fans of Astrology, the Enneagram and other divination tools that can help you understand yourself at a deeper level. I firmly believe that these external modalities are important in our journey *and* that we must also discern when we are becoming attached to a title or description of who we are that's outside of our inner knowing.

The biggest part of this pillar is self-reflection. It's about harnessing the personal responsibility and self-leadership to move from awareness into action. And from there, to actually align our lives to our authentic truth and desires.

Which leads us into the second pillar…

PILLAR 2: SELF-HONORSHIP

This pillar is the bridge between the awareness of knowing who you are and outwardly expressing and owning who you are. This is where your self-trust, self-leadership and personal responsibility are required most.

Self-Honorship is where your conviction is needed so you don't fall back into your limiting patterns of past behavior.

. . .

Self-Honorship is where you make the decisions, create the boundaries and set the standards for who you're being and how you're engaging with the world around you.

Self-Honorship is where you declare those big desires and commit to trusting yourself and your intuitive guidance over everything else. It's your integrity of self-knowership in action.

While using this pillar, you'll notice yourself choosing to be selfish with your time, attention and energy. And you'll recognize that when you're leading from an authentic place, you're actually giving your highest quality service to those around you.

It's important to know that your people pleasing tendencies will surface as you practice these pillars. Each time, you'll be given the choice to bend your boundaries, or honor your desires. It's in the self-honorship that you gain confidence and conviction, and as a result, start seeing the universe respond differently to the energy you're emitting. You can say you want something until you're blue in the face, but if who you're being, and how you're honoring yourself doesn't align with the desired result, your desire will struggle to materialize. It's through the honoring of who you are that you declare to the universe you're able to physically, mentally, emotionally and spiritually hold all that you claim to want.

The best way to start honoring yourself is to look for the frustrations or complaints that are currently present in your life and business. What decisions are you making from a place of should, FOMO (fear of missing out), obligation or pleasing others? Where are you sacrificing what you know to be true for you to make others more comfortable in your presence? Where are you hiding parts of your authenticity for fear of being judged or rejected? Where are you not holding yourself to higher standards, living behind excuses and circumstances? Again, this work requires radical honesty, self-compassion and grace and you move through years of conditioning. It's not a one-and-done deal. This pillar requires continual awareness and refinement of your level of self-honorship, because as you grow and evolve, so will your boundaries, standards and desired priorities. This is the piece that's often forgotten about because as humans, we naturally do what we've always done because we've always done it. We must interrupt the habitual patterns and continue to pair the self-knowership and self-honorship to ensure it reflects our present authentic expression. If we ignore this part of the process, we'll continue to manifest more of what we don't want, because we are moving from a past version of ourselves, not the current truth of our desires. Which leads us into our third and final pillar, self-ownership.

PILLAR 3: SELF-OWNERSHIP

Although the previous two pillars are where most of the *work* takes place, it's in the expression of our self-ownership that we really bring our magic and power together. Self-Ownership allows you to feel the freedom and liberation of your expression, so you can call-in all you desire to be, do, receive, experience, see and feel in your life and business. We've all heard, "we attract who we are." Who we are can be expressed in the two different types of self-ownership that impact this code: *internal* self-ownership and *external* self-ownership.

Internal Self-Ownership:

· · ·

Internal Self-Ownership is the shit that goes on behind-the-scenes in the privacy of your own psyche. It's how you talk to yourself. It's what you make things mean. It's the awareness of where you're giving your power away to external circumstances and specific people or places in your life. We all have internal chatter we must navigate as we move through life and business.

Pay attention to where you're living in victim mode, where you're hiding behind excuses and fears, where you're allowing your results (or lack of results) to create stories or feelings of shame, embarrassment or guilt. Notice where you're absorbing fears and limitations of others, as your own. Notice where you're sacrificing your own impact in the anticipation of disappointment. And a big one in terms of manifesting, the time it's taking to receive the manifestation. Where are you creating pressure or expectation around when you "should" have manifested the 'xyz' already?

Bring awareness to what you're making things mean in terms of how you're experiencing life on your journey towards manifesting your desires. Meaning, where are you creating assumptions and expectations, or putting conditions on yourself, other people or the circumstances you're in, in order to be fully expressed? Where are you holding yourself hostage in being and expressing who you are based on what you've made something mean? For example, saying you'll express yourself fully once you've lost 20lbs, or once you've made $10,000 in a month, or when your partner is fully on board.

External Ownership:

. . .

External Ownership is what other people see, hear and experience when they're in your presence. This is the true "expression" of your authenticity you put on display in the decisions you make from what to wear, how to speak, what to say, what to write, what you create and how you create it. It's in the way you invite people into your world to taste and play in your energy and magic. It's in your outward appearance and the tone of your voice, the way you convey your truth and your presence to the world.

External Ownership is how people experience you as a person, leader, wife, mother, sister, daughter, teacher, community member. It's the energetic imprint you leave on the earth, long after your body is gone. Your external expression is where you get to creatively showcase who you are through different mediums. And it's through the expression of your self-ownership that you attract and magnetize your desires, through the embodied energy of your deepest truth.

It's through your unapologetic self-expression that people feel your true authenticity and respond in kind, unexpected ways, because you've made an impact in their life, however small it may seem.

Let me give you some examples:

People at the grocery store who let you go ahead of them in line

The person you pass in the parking lot who smiles bright at you.

. . .

The salesman at the car dealership who offers a discount.

The representative who upgrades your flight to first class.

The soul aligned client who finds you one minute and jumps into your highest level offer the next day.

The leader you love who asks you to be a guest on their podcast.

The server at the restaurant who brings you a free shot or dessert.

The invite you receive to speak at a popular event.

It's *all* of it, the big and the small.

It's your self-expression that draws people and opportunities towards you. Because when you express your leadership with authenticity and integrity, you know what happens next . . .

THE UNIVERSE RESPONDS.

Now listen, I *get* it. Your brain may want to discount everything I've just shared with you. Because it's not a structured step-by-step, do this then that, kind of thing so it must not be effective in manifesting your desires. But I'm proof, this *works*. And my clients are proof that this *works*. When you know, honor and own who the fuck you are, you're living in a state of energetic alignment to receive the things you desire. Period.

. . .

Remember, we're always manifesting. We are always calling something in, so be aware of who you're being, how you're moving, what you're thinking, feeling and expressing, because it all contributes to the frequency you're sharing with the world, and the universe.

When I first started to understand the power our self-expression holds, I realized that all of the pieces of me I thought I needed to hide were actually the things that attracted and magnetized the key people and opportunities that allowed me to grow and expand my business, my way, with what felt like very little effort or work. Not because I wasn't "working," (manifestation is co-creation, which means we are still required to work with the universe to receive) but because I was moving in such an authentic and freeing way, trusting myself, my intuition and my expression, it felt fun, easy and liberating. I was truly responding to the universe in ways that didn't make logical sense. And I continue to do so. Like I said, this manifestation code is one that continually evolves with you. It's one that I tap into over and over again. I'm always looking for where I can refine and redefine each moment to elevate my experience in life and business. It's through this code that I was able to leave the classroom, replacing my full-time teaching income, to go all in on my business, making way more money in way less time.

It's through the embodiment of this manifestation code that I've been able to manifest these incredible experiences:

- Speaking as a guest on multiple podcasts
- Writing for magazines
- Coaching in other big name leaders' communities
- Speaking on stages
- Free upgrades to first class flights
- Attracting long-term soul aligned clients

- Co-authoring a chapter in this book

My desire for you is that you truly get to experience the full power of unfiltered self-expression in this lifetime, and that it opens up the floodgates for you to receive all of your heartfelt desires. I want you to unlock the magic that happens when you realize you get to manifest whatever you want, purely through being yourself. The more you boldly own your unapologetic self-expression, the more freedom you'll feel. It's that simple.

You're already enough.

You're ready now.

It's time to get out there and fucking own it.

CHAPTER 6
THE CODE: COMPASSION FOCUSED MANIFESTATION
MILLI FOX

My whole world imploded in September of my Grade 11 year. My home life was always full of turmoil and chaos, but on this fateful day something happened that I couldn't run away from. My verbally abusive, alcoholic, coke-head step-dad, whom I did not have a good relationship with, had a massive heart attack and died in the ensuite bathroom of our house. I heard my mom scream to call 911 and thought for sure he'd killed himself. I ran up to the bedroom, picking up the cordless phone that had fallen down our spiral staircase on the way, and dialed for help. I rushed in to find the naked, overweight, 52-year-old man that I hated more than anything, face bashed from hitting the wall, dead on the floor, with my frail mother hyperventilating over top of him.

He was gone instantly. No chance of revival. And just like that, boom. My mom was even more incapacitated than before. Leaving me to administer her final chemotherapy shot, with nothing to do but watch her fade even farther into oblivion from the grief of it all. She already had a serious problem with opiates and alcohol, and after my step dad's death it became so much worse. She went through multiple suicide attempts. Once even coming at me with a knife telling me I was digging my own grave. She had to be physically restrained that night before my aunt came and took me away.

I didn't know how to handle or process any of this, no one asked me how I was doing. I felt like I was just scraping by. I was 16. And with no adults in my life "parenting me," I quit everything, all the teams and clubs and councils, and I did the bare minimum in my final year of high school. I just needed to make it through. Luckily, I'd gotten enough advanced and extra credits that I was able to finish my last year simply doing basic courses, otherwise I don't know how I would have managed. My scholarship was already locked in, so nothing else really seemed to matter.

That year I started smoking weed and hanging out with sketchy people. I got my first tattoo at the only parlor that would accept minors (not the nicest, let me tell you). That tattoo was an anchor in my journey. It said (and still says) 'Para Mi Corazon' which means, *"For My Heart,"* a lyric from a song called Penelope by a band called Pinback. The full lyric goes, *"I'm diving down with all my gear in search of a treasure para mi corazon."* It was my promise to myself that I would always follow the truth of my heart, no matter how hard or scary it became.

I made it into my first year of university at Wilfred Laurier in Waterloo, but nothing felt right. It seemed like all I was doing was checking boxes. It wasn't long before I got fed up and decided to burn it all to the ground. I left my long-term boyfriend, quit university and moved to Toronto. My heart was on a mission, my truth was leading me, and I had treasure to find.

・ ・ ・

Picture me at 18, driving my mom's 1996 rusty, loud, black Jetta, listening to CDs of Abraham Hicks cruising down the streets of Toronto. I'd recently seen the movie The Secret for the first time and was enchanted by the idea that I could *create my own reality*. I felt on top of the world. I'd left the identity constraints of my suburban home town and moved to the anonymous big city. I could be anyone I wanted to be. I had my own place, I was making good money as a server and I felt like I could do anything. Windows down, wind in my hair, I felt so powerful.

And on the flip side, I was battling anxiety and depression. My body felt like that of an 80-year-old. I was smoking a ton of weed, partying, and not feeding myself well. I was weak, underweight, having major digestive issues and pushing myself to my limits with no real idea of how to stop. Around that time, I'd ironically become obsessed with self-help. I was catching highs reading every book I could get my hands on in an attempt to find my silver bullet. I wanted to know the exact steps I could take to guarantee I'd meet my full potential in life. I was looking for an escape from the suffering I was trapped in.

My biggest fear was that I was doomed to mediocrity and all of my struggle was going to be for nothing. I was deathly afraid of being a disappointment and a failure. I didn't know my next step and felt so trapped.

I decided to go back to school. I transferred to York University, because my heart was in Toronto, and I began working my way towards my psychology degree. I had a calling, I knew if I could understand people, I could prevent them from turning towards the dark and shadowy path my mother had taken. If I could just understand, I could help them avoid all the pain and suffering

I'd seen. I had a mission again, I had a purpose, and school was easy for me.

So I plugged through and got the degree. I really didn't have a typical university experience though. I treated it very mechanically, went to class and left. It was transactional, there was no joy in the process, and I was still running from my pain by drinking and partying. And when I finished university I was met with a harsh realization. With no more tests to take or boxes to check, I realized that the real world isn't like school at all. You can't walk in, sit down, write a test, get a good grade and just succeed. Life is just not that linear or predictable, it's wild and messy. Success in the real world is much more layered and nuanced. It requires much more than memorization. It calls for emotional intelligence and resilience. I thought because of my book smarts I would ace life, real quick, but man, did I have a steep learning curve.

After I graduated, I didn't know what to do next. I was eager and ready to dig my teeth into life. I didn't want to be stuck in theory and lectures anymore. While I was figuring it all out, I got into personal training, which turned out to be a huge blessing. Remember when I told you that I was weak, underweight and struggling with my digestion? Getting myself into the gym was the beginning of a revolutionary health journey for me. One that helped me realize that I don't just have to take the cards handed to me, I get to choose how I want to play them. My body was just as valuable as my mind, and when I nurtured both, I became even more powerful.

This was around the time that I entered the world of entrepreneurship. As a headstrong, type A, go-getter I had zero desire to take orders from anyone else. Why would I spend my time building someone else's dream when I could build my own? So I started a personal training and nutrition coaching business. But, boy did I struggle.

Those early days in entrepreneurship made it crystal clear to me that my book smarts and perfectionism were not the be-all-end-all I'd believed them to be. I wrapped all of my self-worth up in my ability to succeed in business, and nothing was working. I struggled to make $1000 a month and kept switching directions hoping each change would magically bring in the big bucks. If I just tried it this way, or that way, or did what she was doing, or what he said the magical system was, it might finally work. Behind the scenes I was battling a tumultuous relationship with my mother, and myself. I began drinking and smoking heavily, in secret, trying to run from the pain of admitting how disappointed I was with my life. Still trying to self-help my way out of the hole, to no avail.

I had many come-to-Jesus moments where I looked in the mirror and wondered if I was indeed going down the very path I had done everything to avoid. The truth was, as much as I was trying to be different, I was still sweeping so much under the rug, trying to "fix myself" by looking externally for the solutions.

Then one day I made some choices that threatened to blow up my entire life as I knew it. I teetered right on the edge of losing everything that meant something to me. It was a wake-up call. I knew I was going to have to change if I didn't want to stumble down the same dark path of self-destruction my mom did.

I turned towards therapy, affirmations, mirror-work and journaling. All things I'd known about for years, but had never done consistently. I was the type of person who would read a self-help book, get to the part with the suggested practices and skim over them, either just doing them quickly in my head or breezing right past them completely. I was always looking for knowledge, but never embodying it. When I finally committed to *actually* doing the work, I made some real changes in my life. I left drinking behind and began to rediscover who I was. I started recognizing how much latent self-loathing had been lurking beneath the surface and how it was subconsciously running my life. At first I was mind-boggled and didn't want to own up to it. It didn't make sense. I was so "good on paper," how could I possibly dislike myself, let alone loathe myself?

The truth was I'd been expending so much energy trying to be perfect, that I didn't actually have a clue who *I* was. I was too busy contorting myself into the image of what I thought I should be, that the voice in my head had made me believe that anything less, aka the *real* me, was a huge let down. *"What do you mean I'm worthy by just showing up? No one is going to tolerate that… you have to give in order to receive."* I just couldn't wrap my head around the concept of inherent worth.

I started to acknowledge my perfectionism and leaned into my vulnerability. My previous idea of "strength" was to be as walled off and unemotional as possible. Think 'I Am a Rock,' by Simon & Garfunkel. One of the biggest blessings that came out of this period of my life was discovering the work of Brene Brown, which wholly changed the way I approached my relationship with myself. Her book, The Gifts of Imperfection, became my bible.

I realized how much of my life I was missing out on by constantly trying to get ahead of my negative emotions and managing other people's perceptions of me. I didn't actually know joy. I thought I could minimize my own pain by being harsh and disciplined. I felt like I had to achieve something in order to be worthy. During this time, I was extremely defensive because of all of my perceived inadequacies, and I was suffering greatly.

I think most of us know to some degree that we are our own worst enemy, yet no one really teaches us how to improve the relationship we have with ourselves. We hear that we should practice self-love, but that can feel really foreign when we're coming from a place of deep self-hatred. It can feel like we're trying to put a bandaid on a gaping wound that really needs stitches.

My deepest healing happened when I discovered self-compassion. In particular, the practice of Mindful Self-Compassion as taught by Dr. Kristen Neff. I found her work through a reference inside of The Gifts of Imperfection by Brene Brown and my life was forever changed.

Compassion became the healing balm that I'd been looking for my entire life. It was the sweet, slow practice of accepting myself as I currently was, and learning how to meet my own needs, that finally allowed me to stop resisting myself. It finally sunk in that the world was not my enemy, that I couldn't grip and force and mold myself into a perfect person. As Abraham Hicks would say, "nothing you want is upstream," yet I was realizing I'd spent nearly 30 years of my life paddling with all my might against the current.

It was around this time, I reacquainted myself with manifestation. I'd found a few online coaches that expanded me greatly through their teachings about manifestation and money mindset. This is when I really started to explore my own identity, what I desired and what was possible for me. I started to give myself a lot of permission to be, do and have whatever I wanted. But predictably enough, I tried to be the perfect manifester. The thing about perfectionism is that it runs deep and it's wildly pervasive. Just because you've acknowledged it in one area doesn't mean it's not going to sneak up on you somewhere else. It's honestly like playing whack-a-mole. I thought that because I was now playing in the realm of energy and potential, not logic and reason, my perfectionism wouldn't sabotage me.

As I worked my manifestation practices, I quickly started to feel like there was something wrong with me. I'd get super triggered when I'd read things like *become an energetic match*, or *be in alignment with your desire*. I resented seeing other women's big manifestations. I felt like I must be doing something wrong. I wasn't able to *affirm the limiting beliefs away* in a snap, like they taught. All this love and light left me feeling like my energy wasn't good enough to get the things I wanted, and that there must be something wrong with me because of all the trauma I'd endured as a kid. I was angry and resentful of the people who had it easier in life. What I realized was,

NO ONE WAS TALKING ABOUT MANIFESTING THROUGH TRAUMA.

The only messages I could find were telling me to reach for a "better feeling thought" or to "auto-suggest the doubt away." I was constantly being told to have discipline, be persistent, and focus relentlessly on my burning desire.

• • •

At this time in my life, I'd already begun my coaching career. I was using what I'd learned through my own therapy, spiritual healing and the work of Brene Brown to start teaching other women how to get out of their own way. I was also injecting bits of manifestation into my work, but hadn't fully figured out how to integrate the two.

I realized more and more that the self-compassion and self-acceptance pieces were missing from the manifestation world. There was a ton of teachings being shared online about taking personal responsibility, but nothing to help ease the blame and shame that came along with those who struggled with it. I noticed this yucky, dark, victim-blaming undercurrent that was going unspoken inside this dreamy, weavy, love and light world.

And I knew I had to do something to address it.

So I came up with a manifestation process that deeply integrated the pillars of wholehearted living laced with radical self-compassion and self-acceptance and called it Compassion Focused Manifestation. And I'm going to teach it to you now.

In a world that teaches us to hustle, it may seem strange to think of compassion and acceptance as part of the manifestation equation. But, dang, if I had a nickel for everytime someone told me that they were finally able to feel the way they wanted to feel after manifesting through my method, I'd be a very rich woman. And in a way, I already am, because I charge a lot more for these teachings than a nickel. You're lucky!

Let me break my process down for you.

. . .

First and foremost, my approach places a lot of emphasis on the different levels of your identity. You can't employ these concepts if you don't consider your relationship to yourself. We need tobe on a journey of self-awareness before we can truly accept and have compassion for ourselves.

The three levels of your identity are:

1. **Your Source Identity**: This is your OG consciousness or what some like to call your soul.
2. **Your Human Identity**: This is your personality, which is all of the dust and sparkle you pick up along your journey on this earth
3. **Your Vortex Identity**: This is the highest most resourced version of you that's already living your dream life.

Let's break them down further.

YOUR SOURCE IDENTITY

Your Source Identity is the one you were born with. Think of God, or the universe or whatever you call your version of a higher power, as the sun, and you as a ray of light emanating from this sun. You are forever inseparable from the most powerful creative source that exists. There is nothing that can alter this connection. It's constant. But many of us have forgotten it. We believe that we are separate, but it's an illusion of the mind. A lapse in memory. Luckily our Source Identity can be easily, and sometimes even instantly recalled.

. . .

The reason why your Source Identity is so important in this manifestation process is that it takes the pressure solely off your human shoulders. If we can remember that we have access to infinite creative power, we can tap into the magic that's always available and stop trying to force our human self to work so hard. We can also ground into this part of our identity when we are deepening our self-acceptance because we know that at our Source Identity level, we are always exactly the way we're meant to be.

How to get in touch with your Source Identity

Connecting with your Source Identity is about going inward. It's about getting still and connecting with something deeper and greater than what appears to the naked eye. I suggest doing things like going into nature and observing the awe that exists there and feeling your connection to it. Also tools like meditation and connecting with your breath through breathwork techniques or simply mindful breathing, can help you connect with the source energy within you. You can also just get quiet and ask yourself, what would make me feel more connected with something bigger than me? What would make me feel more connected with all the other consciousness that exists as an extension of me? See what comes up. Trust yourself. Maybe it's dance, maybe it's swimming, maybe it's a cuddle with your kids or pets.

YOUR HUMAN IDENTITY

This is the layer most people tend to get stuck in when it comes to manifesting. Our Human Identity is the one that gathers up all of our coping mechanisms and past hurts and uses them to behave in ways that once may have served us but no longer do. Our Human Identity is the one with all the quirks and kinks. It's also the one we put the most pressure on, and the one that we tend to devalue the most.

In the modern manifestation world, there's a lot of demeaning rhetoric around the human self or the 3D, mechanical self, which I actually find to be quite harmful. In truth, our Human Identity should be honored. Our Human Identity is the one that needs the most compassion. You can think of your human self almost as your soul-child. If you're a parent, you know how easy it is to be hard on our children for their shortcomings because we project so much of our own insecurities and limiting beliefs onto them. When in reality, our children need to be met where they're at, and cherished for who they are in order to thrive.

Our Human Identity is in a constant battle between its ego and its truth. Imagine it to be a mother with a heavy load, she doesn't need more pressure, she needs acknowledgement, relief and to be told she's doing a great job.

How to get in touch with your Human Level Self

Getting in touch with your Human Identity is about getting to know your preferences. And this can be really fun. Connecting with your Human Identity is discovering what makes you feel good and how you best express yourself. This can be about exploring hobbies, fashion, music, dance. A really simple way to start here is to dip your toe into any of these categories, tune in and ask, do I like this or not? Go shopping, don't buy anything, just look and ask yourself, "do I like this? yes or no?" Try new things, try things you used to like but have let fall to the wayside. Try things that you have always wanted to try. What are your opinions? What are your values? Discover who your human self is now.

How to get in touch with the Shadow Side of your Human Level Self

The shadow side of your human self is more than worth exploring. This is where the radical self-acceptance part of the code comes into play. Sometimes when we hear the word shadow, we automatically associate it with our dark, bad and shameful parts. But the truth is, it's actually quite the opposite. Our shadow shows us all the places within us that are simply looking for love. It shows us the parts of us that we now get to re-parent, bring into the light and re-integrate into our identity to help return us to wholeness. To tap into the Shadow of your Human Identity, reflect on what aspects of yourself you feel bad about. Then take on the perspective of that part. Ask it what it's trying to accomplish, what outcome is it trying to create? Can you view that part of you as endearing? Can you love it for what it brings to the table? Can you find a way to meet its needs in a way that feels juicy and delicious?

YOUR VORTEX IDENTITY

Your Vortex Identity is your aspirational self. It's your favorite version of you. It's who you imagine yourself to be. Unfortunately, what happens with this part of your identity is that it gets far too externalized and idealized. What I mean by that is it gets made into a "perfect" version of you in the mind of your Human Identity. And then that perfect version of you is projected onto your human self, by your human self.

. . .

That's not what this is. Your Vortex Identity is always inside of you. It's the most heart-centered, trusting, aligned with your truth, version of you that's deeply connected to source. It's not "perfect" by any means.

Oftentimes when we try to connect with this version of ourselves we end up trying to be someone we're not. We play dress up and start trying on behaviors and ways of being that don't feel true. I do want to disclaim that there's nothing wrong with playing around with different identities, that can be really healing and helpful in our manifesting. What I'm cautioning you is to be very honest with yourself about your intention while you are attempting to *be her now*. My belief is that the best way to tap into your Vortex Identity is to first connect to your Source identity and pull her forth from that. You can do this through play, but you can also do this by connecting to your highest values and cultivating behaviors (like self-compassion) that are in alignment by choosing to include those actions in your day-to-day life.

How to get in touch with your Vortex Identity

As I mentioned, when most people tap into their Vortex Identity, they end up pretending to be somebody that doesn't feel authentic. Traditional manifestation techniques teach us to make up some sort of future fictional character of who we want to be in order to tap into our highest potential. But I'd like to suggest something different here. First go inwards, into your heart. Tap into the values that you explored in your Human Identity and go from there.

If you were the most resourced version of you (emotionally, spiritually, physically) how would you show up in your day to day? If you had no limitations on your preferences or beliefs, who would you be surrounding yourself with and what would you be creating? If someone was going to write a movie about your life, from the end, how would they be writing your character? How would she play, how would she feel, what kind of questions would she be asking you right now?

Now that we understand the three distinct identities and how to tap into them, we can uncover the next layer of this manifestation code: daily practice. To start, I recommend asking yourself these three questions every day.

1. What are my priorities?
2. What are the actions that will move the needle most towards these priorities?
3. What would feel juicy and delicious for me right now?

Sometimes these things all line up and the priorities get to feel juicy and delicious, and sometimes the juicy and delicious things are separate pieces that I need to consciously inject into my day to support me achieving my priorities. Sometimes we need to step away from the tactical to bring more magic into our lives so that we can refresh our energy.

Next it's important to know how to rise to meet life's inevitable daily challenges. On our manifestation path, problems and setbacks do arise, we are human beings. There are days where I feel like I'm not doing enough or where I get triggered by someone else's behavior. This is life. And this is where the next piece of the manifestation code comes in: self-compassion.

SELF COMPASSION

Self-compassion has had the most profound impact on my life. Research has shown that cultivating self-compassion can be more powerful and effective than cultivating self-confidence, as self-confidence usually involves a fake-til-you-make-it approach that can lead to a false conflation of the self, in other words, overconfidence.

Dr. Kristin Neff, an associate professor of educational psychology at the University of Texas, states that the opposite of overconfidence is self-compassion. She defines self-compassion as: *Treating yourself with the same kindness, care and concern that you would a loved one.* It's framed in terms of humanity, which makes a huge difference when the message of mainstream manifestation is basically to try to forget you're human.

Dr. Neff has influenced my life massively through her work on Mindful Self-Compassion and the concepts she teaches inside her body of work.

Mindful Self-Compassion consists of three elements:

1. Self Kindness
2. Common Humanity
3. Mindfulness

We can use each of these along our manifestation journey to bring us back into a state of wholeness, release resistance and return to our flowing, creating, receiving selves. Here's how I recommend using each one.

SELF KINDNESS

Self Kindness involves cultivating our capacity to extend the same amount of care towards ourselves that we extend towards others. It's about offering ourselves warmth and unconditional acceptance, as well as actively learning how to comfort and soothe ourselves. One of the best ways that we can practice self-kindness is simply asking ourselves, *"What do you need, sweetheart?"*

COMMON HUMANITY

Common Humanity is the sense of interconnectedness that we feel with other people. It's a recognition of the beauty in our human experience and an acknowledgement that all humans, including us, are flawed, works-in-progress. It leans into the fact that as hard as life can be, we are never truly alone and we are all equally made of strength and struggle. No one on earth escapes hardship. Pain is a part of the human experience and any moment of suffering that we have can be transformed into an opportunity for connection with others, and therefore a sense of feeling seen and belonging.

One of the best ways to practice this part of self-compassion is to intentionally seek communities where it's safe for you to be seen and vulnerably share your heart there. Look for spaces where there are people on similar growth and healing journeys to you and where acceptance and compassion are highly regarded values.

MINDFULNESS

Mindfulness is a commitment to being open to things as they are in the moment, in a balanced way. The biggest takeaway I've personally had from learning about mindfulness is finding balance. It means paying attention to our tendencies to over-identify with, or to deny our emotions. Neither of these options are healthy, so we use mindfulness to be radically honest with ourselves about whether we are sweeping things under the rug or allowing ourselves to be taken over and carried away by our emotional experiences.

The best way to do this is to start getting really good at reality checking yourself. I've found having an arsenal of questions to ask yourself is the most helpful way to do this. I personally use and often recommend The Work by Byron Katie as a great place to start.

SELF ACCEPTANCE

The final piece of this manifestation code is Self-Acceptance. Because at the heart of Self-Compassion lies acceptance. In the past whenever I heard someone talking about Self-Acceptance, I always thought it meant giving up. I figured if you were going to accept yourself that meant that you were done with growth and it was all downhill from there. I was definitely not game for this idea. Nope. Not me, with my growth mindset for life.

I didn't realize that by thinking this way, I was approaching my growth journey from a lack mindset. I was viewing myself through a scarcity lens and the truth is, if we are going to manifest anything, we have to do it from a place of sufficiency, not lack.

I had to stop viewing myself as something that was broken and required mending. I wasn't a weekend DIY project, I was a human being. As long as I was unwilling to accept myself, I'd never be able to witness myself as the woman who already had her dream life. I had to stop spending so much energy trying to get rid of all the parts of me that I thought were holding me back and learn to accept them unconditionally.

The truth is, those parts of me that I felt were holding me back were also trying to protect me. They were trying to keep me safe and to meet a need that I hadn't been able to meet in other ways. By trying to banish these parts of myself and approaching them from a place of shame, I was creating more resistance. The opposite of acceptance *is* resistance.

What helped me most in this area was discovering the concept of Existential Kink, which is a process found in a book with the same title by a woman named Carolyn Elliot.

The idea behind the process is to find your low-key, kinky, enjoyment of all the parts of you that you've deemed unacceptable on the surface. It actually plays into the therapeutic process called Internal Family Systems (another process I've found extremely helpful in my self-acceptance journey), where we recognize the benefit that these parts of us bring.

For me, my example was acknowledging my inner "Spoiled Little Bitch". I didn't grow up well off and always was taught to work very hard for what I got and never ask for more than what you need or "deserve." So when I finally found myself in a life where I was receiving more than I ever had before, I found myself very uncomfortable with being able to acknowledge it, or even show gratitude for it, because it was a huge mirror reflecting back my own unworthiness. I had words like spoiled, gold-digger, ungrateful and entitled thrown at me (some of my worst nightmares).

. . .

Then when I discovered the work around Existential Kink, I realized how much latent pleasure I was actually getting from allowing myself to play out this identity. Once I did that, the triggers around being called those names, and the fears associated with them started to dissipate. I was able to receive with much more grace and gratitude.

On top of all that, once I released the resistance around this part of my identity, I actually had a much easier time bringing in more abundance directly through *me* instead of having it provided for me, indirectly.

As you can see, doing the excavation work that comes with self-acceptance can have very wide reaching and powerful effects that we might not even anticipate. But if we can just begin connecting the dots and start recognizing that the more WHOLE we are, the less resistance we fall into, and the more our dreams and desires can flow with ease and beauty.

It's really not about *making* manifestation happen, it's about removing all the obstacles that are standing in our way of simply receiving. It's about recognizing the shame speed bumps and potholes that exist on our journey and being mindful enough to not fall into them multiple times. We can do that by using these manifestation codes.

WHERE THESE MANIFESTATION CODES HAVE TAKEN ME:

These manifestation codes have taken me from being a hyper-anxious, extreme perfectionist with painfully low self-worth to a woman who *trusts* herself, feels held and proud, and has the results to show for it.

Since I've implemented these changes in how I relate to myself I've been able to manifest the most beautiful things that life has to offer, things that go way beyond the 'blingy' vision board stuff.

Let me remind you of what my life looked like right before I dove deeply into this work. I was struggling to make $1000 a month in my business. I felt like I was "checking all the boxes," and everything seemed so hard. I couldn't understand why nothing was falling into place for me. I constantly felt like I was trying to prove something. I constantly got defensive. I was feeling desperate and plagued by my perception that I was still a "failure" even though I knew I had so much potential. I was exerting so much effort trying to get it all right, and I just felt so tired. I felt like I was living a lie, going on vacations, living in beautiful places, and doing extraordinary things, but I never feeling worthy of any of it.

But once I started to embody these manifestation codes, things started to flow and feel easy in my life. I was able to find so many moments of relief and solace in my new tools and practices. I started to feel worthy of what I already had, and was finally able to feel gratitude for my life as it was instead of feeling shame and undeserving of it.

Since I made these shifts, I have skyrocketed my business. I've had $30k sales months, and rarely dip below $8k. I purchased myself a luxury vehicle, and I'm completely financially self-sufficient. To be honest though, while all of that is a huge accomplishment, I think the other things I've been able to manifest and change in my life are much more important and hold a lot more meaning to me.

Firstly, I was able to have the best year of my entire relationship with my mom before she passed away in early November of 2022. I also healed my relationships with so many of my other family members as a result of our reconciliation, including many aunts and cousins that I felt estranged from. And my relationship with my brother and my dad are better than they've ever been.

I've been holding myself in my grief for my mom's passing in the most beautiful and inspiring ways. I'm witnessing the ways I'm treating myself, speaking to myself and allowing myself to move through all the emotions and places I need to in order to process this very huge and complex thing for me.

As I mentioned earlier in the chapter, my relationship with my mom was not an easy one, and that has made losing her even more complex. There is so much that comes with losing a parent, especially when you have so many mixed feelings tied up in the relationship. A parent is your foundation in life and whether they're a sturdy one or not, taking that foundation away rocks you. So my work now has been steadily building my own foundation and re-grounding myself in my new life.

I've also spent more than the majority of my adult life dedicating myself to being a cycle breaker. I've made it my mission to be the first woman in my family line to live from a place of wholeness and joy, breaking the cycles of abuse and addiction that have plagued my ancestors for generations. My mom's death opened up the space for me to process the part of my Human Identity that I inherited from her, and all the stories she passed on to me about being a survivor. I now get to evolve my identity to a place where I'm no longer dependent upon or fueled by those stories. There is no way I'd be able to hold myself here without these manifestation codes.

To finish it all off, in January of 2023, my husband of 9 years and I began our official process of separation. Another huge part of my identity began shifting and I'm being met with a whole new load of emotions to process. And while this is still very fresh for me, I've already managed to build so much more trust in the universe about what's possible because of these manifestation codes. I've been moving through higher highs and lower lows than ever, and I don't look at this as a bad thing. I don't view it as a roller coaster, I view it as an expansion. I'm so proud of my capacity to hold space for my own pain and discomfort because it's given me the capacity to hold space for more beauty, joy and gratitude too.

You can't selectively numb. When we learn to hold space for our "negative" emotions, mindfully (i.e. not over identifying with them or shoving them under the rug), we also learn how to allow the joy in without running away from it out of the fear it won't last. Self-compassion and acceptance allow us to really experience the full range of what being human has to offer, we get to have it all, literally, and we get to see the incredible gift and beauty in that.

A lot of people have asked me how I've been able to show up at the level that I have while I've been carrying all of this, and without a second of hesitation I credit these manifestation codes.

. . .

I would have retreated into the darkness and got lost in running and numbing if I didn't learn these processes and build the resilience that they've afforded me. Instead, I am wildly proud of myself. I find moments of massive joy in my day-to-day life. I don't need to seek peak experiences to feel alive, although I still enjoy luxury and very nice things. I don't feel that I have to be living this insanely extraordinary, fancy and bling-y lifestyle to feel like I'm doing something right or that I'm special.

I've tapped into the true power of now, because I know that I AM everything right now. This was a really hard concept for me to wrap my mind around for a long time but I can proudly say that I truly and deeply feel it today, thanks to these manifestation codes.

I hope they unlock the same magic for you, that they have for me.

CHAPTER 7
FINAL THOUGHTS

As you can see, manifestation truly is like art. There is no one-size-fits-all approach to creating the life of your dreams. Every one of us has a unique relationship with the universe. And it's up to us to open up to it.

No matter where you are on your journey, you are powerful. You are capable. You have what it takes to create a masterpiece with your life. Manifestation is available to each and every one of us. The women inside this book are not special. They've struggled, doubted and lost. They are human beings just like you. And yet, they've been able to create extraordinary lives through the embodiment of their Manifestation Codes.

My suggestion to you now that you've read this book is to practice and experiment! Choose the codes that speak to you and begin to weave them into your daily life. Try them on. See how they feel. Watch what they create. And adapt your manifestation process as you go along. With an open heart, a little faith and a creative mind, there truly is no limit on what you can create and experience. Happy Manifesting!

CHAPTER 8
TIME FOR THE WORLD TO MANIFEST

A s you align your mindset, behaviours and actions with your manifestations, you put yourself in an excellent position to inspire someone else.

Simply by leaving your honest opinion of this book on Amazon, you'll show new readers where they can find the codes they need to manifest a life of their dreams.

Thank you so much for spreading the word. You're on the path to manifest what you desire – and you can inspire someone else to do the same.

>>> Click here to leave your review on Amazon.

Hyperlink ">>> Click here to leave your review on Amazon." with **your** review link for the eBook version.

. . .

Replace ">>> Click here to leave your

ABOUT THE AUTHORS

LISA FERNANDES

Lead author and publisher, Lisa Fernandes is a coach and healer who explores new-age thought, energetics, and spiritualism.

Lisa guides readers on a journey to unlock and embrace their true selves, guided by her connection to collective awareness.

Lisa's journey as a collective visionary began when she hit rock bottom. As she clawed herself out of a place of despair, she discovered the path to accepting and understanding herself, reinterpreting qualities she had thought to be failing as the sparks of potential they truly were.

As a publisher, Lisa brings new-age thought to the forefront of her work.

Connect with Lisa << here

ALEXANDRA CARRUTHERS

Alexandra Carruthers is a storytelling + content marketing mentor for intuitive entrepreneurs who want to stand out, sell out and distinguish their voice in their industry.

She guides coaches, creatives, leaders + healers through a journey of activating their authentic tone and unlocking their unique Story Codes. She teaches her clients how to weave their codes into their content and effortlessly sell their services in their own voice, so they become a stand-out authority in their industry. She also helps spiritual entrepreneurs write books. Taking their online teachings and transforming them into timeless publications that expand their field of impact.

Connect with Alex >> here

ANDI TURCZA

Andi is a mother of two, Spiritual Healer & Intuitive Manifestation Coach for women and men that are ready to be the most empowered version of themselves.

Andi's goal is to be the person she needed 10 years ago. She understand all life challenges are unique and complex to all individuals.

    Heal Toxic Relationships
    Reclaim Your Power
    Awaken Your Potential
    Release the Sh*t that's holding you back!

                          Connect to Andi << here

CHARISSA LYNN

Charissa Lynn is an international mentor and psychic visionary who helps women connect to their intuition and soul-led mission. She's a mother of 3 residing in London, Ontario, Canada.

Charissa's purpose is to guide through the use of her own experience and psychic gifts. Her desire is for all women to live their most expansive life and create a soul aligned successful business through both strategy & energetics.

Her passion and legacy is to lead women towards their freedom by creating a new paradigm of wealth for themselves and generations to come, while making an impact on the collective, leaving a positive ripple effect for eternity.

Connect with Charissa >> here

KARI RUSSELL

Kari Russell is an Energetic Business Coach, global leader in Self-Expression and host of the S-EX Talk Podcast.

She is married with 2 children and lives in a small country town just outside Peterborough in Ontario, Canada where you'll find her tanning on her deck reading spicy romance novels in the summer or submerged in her hot tub in the winter.

Kari's coaching centres around Human Design, Mindset, Emotional Intelligence and Identity Work to help her clients release the stories and conditioning that hold them back from expressing themselves unapologetically in life and business.

Her work focuses on fusing the psyche and the somatic to guide her clients in leveraging their authenticity to own who the f*ck they are in their branding and content to make a massive impact, unlock wealth and build their business their way!

Connect with Kari << here

MILLI FOX

Milli Fox is obsessed with all things self-worth and manifestation. Think Brené Brown meets Gabby Bernstein with a sprinkle of goofy on top.

Milli has created a unique process for Manifestation that she's titled Compassion Focused Manifestation, helping women move toward their dream life from a place of wholeness & integrity.

Milli has been called to live a boldly authentic life that reclaims the definition of luxury in order to expand what women believe is possible for them. She aims to raise the collective consciousness and heal generational trauma through her coaching, programs and internet dance parties.

Milli is a 2x's published author and voracious reader- who is currently writing the next NYT bestseller on Manifestation.

Connect with Milli >> here

www.ingramcontent.com/pod-product-compliance
Lightning Source LLC
Chambersburg PA
CBHW060615080526
44585CB00013B/834